Touching the Flame

Touching the Flame

An Enquiry into Deep Desire

Mary Booker

Published in this first edition in 2022 by:
Triarchy Press
Axminster, UK

www.triarchypress.net

ISBNs:

Print: 978-1-913743-68-0
ePub: 978-1-913743-69-7

tp

Contents

Poems

Introduction

Curiosity and desire can be the most precious forces.
Rob Burbea, *Seeing That Frees*

The last decade has been one of the most intense in my life – in a particular sense. Its intensity has not been like the unrelenting loneliness of my childhood, or the excitement and angst of my teens and twenties, or the confusion and exhaustion of my thirties, or the upheaval and reformation of my forties and fifties. The decade of my sixties has been about going deeper down into myself and consequently deeper into life. It has been a time of intense enquiry. Don't get me wrong – I have been enquiring all my life, constantly wondering, learning, questioning, exploring, experimenting, researching, creating – trying to discover what was really going on, what it all means, what my part in it might be. But I now felt the urge to give myself more to deeper enquiry – fuelled by an awareness that the time remaining to me on this earth is becoming increasingly brief. I was, in fact, finally responding to a huge personal desire to be creative and to become more in touch with life.

I began my sixties by giving myself time apart from my normal life – three months in springtime, on my own, at the very edge of Dartmoor. Every day I walked for hours on the moor or in the woods. I took photographs to record what I called "watching the world come alive". I wrote a journal of my thoughts and experiences – and I meditated at least twice, sometimes three times, a day. I came out of it feeling I had a new chance to live – really live – my life. During that time I explored some simple, basic things about myself as an embodied being – when it was that my body wanted to go to sleep, when it wanted to wake up, when and what I wanted to eat, where my feet wanted to take me and when they wanted to stop, and what I wanted to spend time really looking at and listening to. I did not then think of these as within the realm of desire. I was just trying to get to know who I was when not constantly having to respond to the demands of others.

I wanted even more access to life, and so I decided to work through movement – through my living, breathing, moving body – as it seemed to have shown me in those few months that it had relevant ideas about how to be fully alive. I started attending 'Move into Life' workshops[1] with Sandra Reeve, using the movement practice that Sandra introduced me to as a basis of support for both creativity and enquiry. I also gave myself permission to write poetry – something that I had yearned to do since I was a child, but, somehow, seldom had.

My first focused enquiry using this approach was into the experience of ordinary, everyday, but enduring FEAR in my life. The project, which I named *Working Creatively with Fear*, took five years in all and found several expressions. I created a performance around a series of my own poems based on the relationship that some of the characters in Shakespeare's *The Tempest* have with fear. I ran a therapeutic enquiry group on the subject with a group of therapists, and wrote a chapter on this for the European Consortium of Arts Therapy Education[2] after presenting at one of their conferences. The enquiry into fear led almost seamlessly into an enquiry into the experience of VULNERABILITY, and resulted in a book being published of my poetry and photos expressing vulnerability.[3] All this constituted an awakening of intense creativity and I certainly felt enlivened.

But then…where to go next? The idea that came up, seemingly arising naturally from my enquiries into fear and vulnerability, was to address the question of DESIRE. It first arose clearly towards the end of my research into trauma, when I was reading a book called *Awakening the Dreamer: Clinical Journeys* by Philip Bromberg. Bromberg suggests that early difficulties with the infant's ability to satisfy their normal appetite can be the origin of eating disorders later in life.

> *…what in adulthood might have developed into appetite and healthy, regulatable desire, instead, because it is denied the relational context on which that transformation depends, freezes the experience of being an affectively out-of-control infant within a dissociated self-state that takes on an imperious life of its own.*[4]

This immediately and strongly resonated with me around my own very early history, which I believe left me with unresolved issues around eating. I knew I would need to look more deeply at this.

An impaired ability to regulate emotionally is connected with early developmental trauma, which I had been investigating within my fear enquiry. But desire feels so much more than purely physiological urges and appetite. What about the desire to create? To explore? To connect? The desire to enter deeply into life, the mind, the heart? What is my heart's desire? What makes my heart sing? What arises when I ask myself, "What do I really want?"

These questions open up huge areas of exploration and ever more questions. Some other questions that occurred to me as I began were:

- Is desire by nature insatiable? Does it always seek more?
- If desire is for something other, does a sense of lack always accompany it?
- Does a desire sometimes / often / always point to another deeper desire? Is there any end to this?
- Does desire always lead to suffering, as seems to be indicated in Buddhist thought?
- Is desire essential to life?
- Desire is highly motivating. How best to access such energy of motivation?
- Why do illness and depression seem to remove desire from my life? Is this because they are too absorbing?
- What is the relationship between desire and vulnerability?

What follows is an account of my enquiry into these and other questions around desire – always attempting to move deeper to discover for myself what it is that I really want in this life. I will intentionally not be providing answers to most of my questions. Enquiry is the thing. Michel de Montaigne is considered the father of the art of essay writing.[5] He would ask big questions and then allow himself to follow the different threads and pathways those questions took him along. Definitive answers are not so important to me, feeling too close-ended; while resonances, patterns and connections are stimulating. There will be a degree of wandering up different pathways in this enquiry, although I hope to organise my ramblings enough to enable you to follow the sense of it. We all create our own meanings but my hope is that what I discover will, in some ways, also be meaningful to others.

It is good to first acknowledge some of the lenses through which I will be viewing desire. My approach to enquiry is basically phenomenological. I am interested in both the experience of desire and what it means. Desire requires there be something that is desired. Husserl, the founder of phenomenology, proposed what he called "intentionality" in terms of perception and experience. In this sense, desire arises because of our fundamental intentionality – that is, we turn what we perceive into something. We can then construct a meaning for that thing and have a relationship with it.[6] Our relationship with any object of desire is crucial to our experience of desire.

My perceptions of, and meanings around, desire will be unique to me, although hopefully there will be sufficient shared elements for others to relate to, whatever their background. I will be looking at how the personal experiences and encounters in my past have affected my experience of desire. Our culture shapes our experience, including our experience of desire, and I need to acknowledge my white, Anglo-American, educated, middle class background. I am especially interested in the cultural lens of my being a woman. There are ways to view desire within philosophy and psychology and, as these have been part of my education and livelihood, I will be dipping into some of them. Another important influence that has arisen in my life is Buddhism, and I will be looking at desire through a few different Buddhist lenses. I spent my childhood in the beautiful countryside of upstate New York, and now live in verdant Devon, so the important, on-going relationship I have with the natural world informs any enquiry I embark on, and desire is no exception.

To aid this enquiry, I started an on-line blog called Going Deeper[7] where I could share some of my thoughts and have others respond. I again enlisted the support of Sandra Reeve and fellow movement practitioners. I wanted to move with my desire as well as think, read and write about it. Desire is experienced emotionally and emotion is first-and-foremost visceral - in the body as well as the mind.

If I put desire into the alchemical vessel, will its golden essence be found? With that approach it's very easy to end up with fool's gold. Perhaps it's not a matter of finding essential desire, but of seeing and opening up to the complexity of desire. Recently I have been introduced to Nora Bateson's view of systems theory and learning which she calls "symmathesy" - *the process of contextual mutual learning through interaction.*[8] She is interested in engaging with and learning from the actual complexity of our world and experience, rather than trying to reduce the problems we face down to answers and solutions. She proposes that all living systems (not just us humans) are sense-making, that we need to study things without taking them out of their contexts which are continually changing, and that in order to 'do' complexity we need to understand our own complexity.[9] Desire is complex – and rather than separate it out too much and pin it down in order to study it, I will attempt to look at desire within some of the contexts that occur to me. I want to open the conversation up, rather than narrow it down. I am also aware that simply by focusing on certain questions and looking from certain angles, I am breaking up the complexity, hoping my awareness of symmathesy compensates a bit for this.

LOOKING FOR DESIRE

Bless the spirit that makes connections, for truly we live in what we imagine.
Rainer Maria Rilke, *Sonnets to Orpheus*

NEEDS AND DESIRE

There are basic needs and drives – for food, sex, safety, security, a sense of self-worth and so on. But there is a blurring that occurs between need and desire. When we ponder the two, we might sense a difference, like when a parent asks a child who is fervently demanding something, "Is it a need or a want?" Of course, if they strongly desire it, they will respond, "I **need** it!" Often we experience our desires as needs. In the 1940s Abraham Maslow proposed what he called a hierarchy of needs, beginning with physiological needs, then safety needs, followed by belonging and love needs, then esteem needs and topped by what he called self-actualisation needs which include creativity and spiritual development. This model is usually set out as a triangle, with the basic needs at the broad bottom, rising upwards through the different levels towards the point of self-actualisation. Rising is the opposite of my own view of a deepening. I am also suspicious of there being a tip to the triangle which suggests there is some end point you can ascend to, like the summit of a mountain. I prefer to do away with any suggestion of separation between the different levels, as there could be seen to be a number of needs/desires in play at any one time. What level might you be on when you are hungry and need to eat, and also desire to create something really lovely to eat? Of course, if you are genuinely starving, you will just grab the nearest edible thing. Circumstances, including culture and upbringing, will not only dictate how basic your needs might be but also how you interpret these needs. But maybe desire arises out of need? Where and when does what we experience as desire begin?

I acknowledge that there are certain baseline survival needs and drives, both physical and emotional, underpinning desire, but the potential for confusion is present even in this. For instance, the overlap in desire imagery between food and sex has often been noted. The connection between fear and desire can be seen in some of the following dysfunctional relatives in the desire family. When basic needs/drives are frustrated or damaged, they can lead to problematic desires, often experienced as basic, intense needs, connected with:

- Addictive behaviours including substance addiction

- Obsessions, including sexual obsessions
- A focus on worldly desires such as for wealth, power, conquest, fame, etc.
- Longing: It seems to me this is not as able to motivate action as desire is. It even can lead to chronic inaction. Pothos was one of the Erotes[1] and symbolised longing or yearning. It's interesting that his flower was one that was used at funerals. Are we in the realm of Freud's Thanatos?
- A focus on physical pleasure/hedonism: Might this be a distraction or escape from facing inevitable mortality?

Beyond survival, maybe it is how we perceive a want that determines whether it is a need or a desire for us. What's its story? Or rather, what kind of story are we telling ourselves about it? The connection between what Husserl termed intentionality – the objectifying of our perceptions – and desire was mentioned in the Introduction. There are all kinds of unconscious filters through which our mind sieves our perceptions, so that we only give our attention to those that are 'important'. We turn what we perceive into things, so that we can tell ourselves stories about them and make meanings. These stories, or fabrications, are potentially endless and vary from the very simple to the highly elaborate. Many of them are cultural, learned stories. Others arise from our personal experiences. They may begin with basic sensory perceptions (*seeing a hat*) but evolve into more subtle perceptions of feeling and thought (*I like that hat. It reminds me of my mother. The colour is gorgeous, like a night sky. It would be perfect for the wedding*, etc.). This is so complex, and often under the radar of our full awareness, that it is impossible to take a desire out of its context, which will include all the perceptions of what is seen as outside us and what is experienced as inside us. This book is really full of stories about desire. It cannot be otherwise.

A story of mine where the experience of desire is muddled with unmet need is around food. I have had difficulties with impulsive, emotional eating, often when I am tired, or when I am living in my head and disconnected from my body, or when I am unhappy, frustrated, anxious or angry. I am one of millions who suffer from this. There are so many of us you might as well call it normal. But it can be humiliating be thrown out of control so frequently around food, and this is made worse by the pressures and shame our culture projects onto bodies and appetite, particularly women's. Ever since knowing the circumstances of my birth, I have felt my eating issues were rooted in my birth experience and then compounded by my relationship with my not-quite-available mother as I grew up. This is the story that makes sense to me, and also gives me a handle on how I might relate to this desire in a less painful and unhelpful way. I have written about my birth and my mother elsewhere[2] but, in a nutshell, I was separated from her in hospital at my birth and brought to her every four hours for "ten minutes a side" – then firmly taken away from her again and put in a room full of isolated babies. My father was away and the hospital wouldn't let my mother go home until he returned two weeks later. Two weeks is an eternity to a baby and this regime had its effects. My mother said by then I was "a very good baby", meaning I didn't make any fuss. In my childhood, while she was providing my food (and she was very good at this), I remained unaware of any impulsive eating. But I did suck my thumb (a lot) until I was 12 years old when shame at the behaviour finally out-weighed the desire. I also went through a period in late childhood of stealing – mostly little things from five & dime stores that I didn't even want. The shame I felt every time was excruciating. This came to an end when I stole $5 from my mother's purse. She asked me about it and I denied knowing anything, but the unbearable shame about lying to my beloved (if unobtainable) mother brought an end to my stealing. Here in my personal story, I am noticing a connection between desire and shame.

It was when I left home and started feeding myself that the sense of a lack of control around eating began to be felt. I have found various ways of managing my weight through my adult life – but, until recently, not a way of managing the feelings of shame and being out of control around certain foods (usually fatty, sweet things). I was breastfed, and honour my mother in her insistence on this against the prevailing culture of the time. Having breastfed my own children, I now know how sweet breast milk tastes. Sweet is a very primal taste and is associated with feeling nourished, relaxed and held – but indulging in sweet foods doesn't really provide that, does it? At least not for long. It's been like this: I'm driving home from a long day and know I will be passing a shop. The desire-thought for a Snickers bar arises in my mind (a neat package of sweet, fat and protein – like breast milk). I recognise it and think I've got a handle on it. I try to let what arises in my mind just flow through me: *You deserve it after such a hard day!* – the taste memory arises – *You're too weak to stop yourself, aren't you!* – I smell the Snickers bar. But I then remind myself about how bad I will feel afterwards, both physically and emotionally, and tell myself that what I really need is a couple of wholemeal crackers and a cup of tea, followed by a 15 minute lie-down. Yes – I am almost home and relax a bit. Suddenly someone else takes control of the car and of me, and I am turning into the local shop, getting out, buying a Snickers bar and eating it immediately in the car. I drive home feeling defeated and humiliated – but also sort of satisfied. This sense of satisfaction I now see as coming from the exiled, hungry, angry infant inside. The needs of the infant, morphing into desire, have taken me for a ride.

Having found a story about my desire that I could understand and relate to, I basically used my imagination, with therapeutic support, to re-connect with that needy and very angry infant inside me, who was cut off from my consciousness. It is an ongoing relationship now, one that requires regular attention. But addressing this desire has transformed my ability to relate to my desire in general by shedding the cloak of shame. I can now allow myself to enjoy my food desires without going into shame – like for raspberries and dark chocolate. I can indulge my infant self at times, without her taking me for a ride. And I can keep finding ways to connect – to try to heal the foundational experience of disconnection.

I am curious about how non-humans experience desire. Like Mary Oliver in her poem, *Some Questions You Might Ask*,[3] where she challenges assumptions about who or what might possess a soul, I question assumptions about who or what might experience desire. Is there a blurring between need and desire for them too? Anyone who has watched a dog begin to wriggle and dribble when it sees someone holding a treat understands that the dog is engaged in perception, has formed some kind of story in its mind about the object in the hand, and desires it. Then, think of a deer grazing. It has some consciousness of self and other, for instance perceiving a predator as not-deer and to be avoided. And it has preferences for what it eats, seeking out the most succulent foods around rather than just eating whatever is in front of it. This seeking could be said to indicate desire. Higher mammals clearly have intentionality and also seem to experience desire in some form. Even a slug appears to have preferences it seeks out. But does a tree desire? I can hardly imagine what a tree's desires might be, but I really don't want to discount the possibility – a tree version of pleasure as it turns its leaves to the light. They certainly have perceptions – and they respond in quite complex ways.[4] Maybe non-humans just play on the desires of others in order to get their needs met.

Lemon Desires

This lemon wants to have my attention – and it does.
It wants me to break open its bright yellow skin.
As I do, my desire increases with its
only-possible-as-lemon scent.
Its desire meets and engages my desire.
We are in a mutual desire relationship.

This lemon wants its seed released
to germinate, to reach for the warmth,
then the light of the sun.

This lemon wants to express its treeness –
to root, branch, leaf and blossom –
to open its blossom, exude nectar and pollen –
to arouse the desire of bees.
The exotic, erotic blossom desires to pollinate
and be pollinated.

This lemon embraces the desire of
seed, tree and blossom to fruit –
and requires the whole cosmos
for its fulfilment.
I desire to be a willing participant
in this relationship of desire –
to see, to touch, to hold, to smell,
to break into, to taste –
too sour!

So, how to delineate between need and desire? This is difficult as both are hugely motivating and bring energy with them, both can involve a sense of lack, and they can be inextricably intertwined with each other. I feel a need to understand my desire. I can only try to identify desire for myself, knowing it may not fit others' experience. Needs can, at least hypothetically, be satisfied – desire is always up for more. For me, desire has some sense of deliciousness about it – moving me sometimes right down into my core. There is a combination of emotional, visceral and sensual arousal. I also find it often involves some kind of experience of beauty and pleasure. The beauty does not have to be of a conventional kind, but nonetheless it is there. Thinking about an object of desire will bring a smile to my face and a warmth to my heart. There is a fieriness – passion – and often a sense of letting go of control in some way. I am remembering the wonderful and funny sex scene in the 1989 film, *The Tall Guy*[5] – two people trashing a room in their equal desire for each other. And, as I hope to show, desire does not have to be grounded in lack.

MOVING – DESIRE AS A VERB

Desire moves. Eros is a verb.[1]

In an attempt to clarify for myself what desire might be, beyond the arena of basic need, I picked up my ancient, yellowing, well-thumbed Thesaurus[2] and found the below, which I turned into a poem.

> **To Desire** – *a found poem*
>
> To wish, wish for, care for, affect,
> like, take to, cling to, fancy.
> To prefer, have an eye to, have a mind to.
> To have a fancy for, have at heart, be bent upon.
> To set one's heart (or mind) upon,
> covet, crave, hanker after, pine for, long for.
> To hope, etc.
> To woo, court, ogle, solicit, fish for.
> To want, miss, need, lack, feel the want of.

There are obviously a lot of possible goings-on in desire.

William Irvine[3] suggests that the wellsprings of desire lie in the classic approach/avoidance response – our wanting to feel good and avoid feeling bad. This response can be seen in just about any life form that can move at all – and it is about surviving and thriving. From the Buddhist perspective, this leads to attachment and aversion, both being forms of what is called 'craving'. I intend to explore the Buddhist view of desire later, but, as my poem below indicates, it may be necessary and natural to be pushed beyond avoiding feeling good or bad – and feeling bad may be necessary in order to connect with feeling good. How good it can feel when a pain disappears!

My first response to the question of origin was to consider a primary experience of wanting. Where was it my wanting might initially have been felt? As a foetus in the womb, all my needs would have been met, and wanting might have arisen from the separation experience of birth:

The Birthing of Desire

I want to move!
I want more room – more space!
I want this squeezing to stop!
I want the hurting to stop!

I want the warmth I have lost!
I want the holding I have lost!
I want the sounds I have lost!
I want the soft light, soft dark I have lost!
I want the place of just being I have lost!

Is anyone there?
I want you.

Is wanting the same as desiring? In current use it seems to be, but my daughter-in-law pointed out that the way we regard the word 'want' has changed from the original sense of lacking something required or essential to a more self-centred 'having a desire to possess'.[4] This possibly reflects the increased value that we now give to being an individual rather than part of a collective, which has arisen over historical time. But do either of these actually encompass what desire can be?

Irvine looks at the connection between desire and motivation, seeing that some types of desire are far more motivating than others. His conclusion is that hedonic desire (clearly emotional) is far more motivating than non-hedonic desire (seemingly intellectual). The intellect tends to form "instrumental desires" that lead towards something more rooted in emotion. There are "chains of desire" in which it can be hard to determine the origin. But if there is motivation then there is emotion. He points out that 'emotion' and 'motivate' come from the same root: *movere*, the Latin for 'to move'. So desire is connected with some kind of movement, be this movement in the direction the mind takes, or in the body's sensations and actions, or in the aroused heart.

If desire is connected to movement, then what happens if I try to embody and move with desire? When I did this, I found my hands and arms repeatedly reaching out – reaching out to some 'other'. Then I found myself remembering how I always reach out to roses. For me roses are like babies. You know how, when a baby comes into a space, every mind and eye turns in their direction – reaches towards the baby. Babies are very powerful in the way they demand our attention. It needs to be this way because they are so vulnerable and need to elicit our care. It is only social constraints that keep me from reaching out to touch, to hold the baby in my arms and smell the sweetness of their soft head. Roses are like babies for me, with fewer social constraints.

Reaching for Roses

I am one of those people
who rudely lean into
other people's gardens,
reaching to draw towards me
a rose.

Wandering through public gardens,
I will visit every rose bush,
stepping into neatly tended borders
to reach the rambling deep red rose
right at the back.

A rose must be a whole experience:
examine the tight bud giving hints of hue,
cup an open blossom in my hand,
stroke the soft petals, then press my face
into this beauty.

Finally – inhale deeply,
with open desire,
the perfume saved to last.

Of course, the reaching out gesture might also relate to the newborn's memory of being separated from the womb and from the mother – but it didn't feel like that when I was moving. I felt it like a delicious opening to.

Why do roses move me so much – both arouse and symbolise desire? Roses have an interesting history in symbolism – both spiritual and sexual. Love, purity, beauty, divinity, passion and desire are all connected to roses. The phrase 'the rose of the soul' comes to me. It is a fundamental flower in Islamic gardens, its scent being particularly important. The rose has been associated in the past with the Greek goddess Aphrodite, as well as with the Virgin Mary. In the language of flowers, a red rose is passionate love. When I ponder what the rose means to me, I am aware of its sensuality and my heart also feels moved. This must be why it has been connected to both spirit and body. There is a tenderness about roses – and there is always the thorn as well. My arms have been well and truly bloodied by my reaching for roses – soft beauty on the briar. But is reaching out my only movement of desire? How does 'reaching out for' become 'opening to'? Contact generating desire for more contact?

LACK AND LONGING

Many who write about desire do so in terms of lack and longing. I certainly can feel this lack and longing, as evidenced by the poem below, written in 2012. But is the desire only in the lack and longing – even here?

Morning Moment

It's not quite 6:30 and I wake from a dream I can't remember –
throw my legs out of bed and turn off the not-yet-ringing
    alarm clock.
It's morning again.
I see a smudge of pink through the leaf patterns on the glass
    in the bathroom window.
Opening it a crack reveals to me broken grey clouds.
It's a splash-the-face-only day.
Downstairs, dressed in a new blue top and with beads
    dripping from my earlobes,
I know the birds are waiting for me in the garden.
Damp grass (rain last night) –
apples and rose petals fallen on the ground.
There it is – that longing –
to enter together with another into the morning scents,
the light – and delight –
blurring into each other's being within the living moment.
Morning moment.
There is no one there.

I remember a moment of sharing my desire with another in a movement workshop. I was really enjoying moving with a lovely, long pink cloth – feeling my desire for, and opening to, the colour – like I do with roses. Someone moved near and whispered, "I want the pinkness!" I shared the pink cloth with him and the more I shared it, the more beautiful it felt. I soon gave him the cloth and I didn't feel I was losing anything. The sharing of the desire seemed to transcend any sense of lack, want, me/mine/my. There was desire without needing to have. Sharing moments of desire and beauty with another can contradict the sense of lack.

The notion of lack as an element of desire keeps coming up. I want to address this because I feel uncomfortable with something as motivating as desire being so closely tied to something as depressing as lack and longing. At times it seems to be so, but at other times, including when reaching for roses, it doesn't fit at all for me. Certainly, in my deepest, most fulfilling experiences of desire, lack and longing don't seem present. During my time on Dartmoor, described in the Introduction, I did not experience any sense of lack or longing – but I was clearly engaging with desire. There had been a sense of longing associated with the original idea of the retreat. I remember walking in a lane at the edges of the moor and thinking, "Wouldn't it be lovely to not go home now – but stay and walk and write for a long time?" So, there was a feeling in my life then of lacking the space to do just that. When I gave myself the space, the sense of lack dissolved, but desire did not.

I find the interweaving of lack and longing confusing in terms of my experience. Certainly longing and desire have a long history together – in story, poetry and song, for instance – and there is both beauty and passion in this. Rebecca Solnit speaks of desire and longing in *A Field Guide to Getting Lost* in a way that echoes the poetics of longing.

> We treat desire as a problem to be solved, address what desire is for and focus on that something and how to acquire it rather than on the nature and the sensation of desire, though often it is the distance between us and the object of desire that fills the space in between with the blue of longing. I wonder sometimes whether with a slight adjustment of perspective it could be cherished as a sensation in its own terms, since it is as inherent to the human condition as blue is to distance?[1]

There is the kind of desire that privileges lack and longing – what has been called "the bittersweet". Anne Carson traces this back to the Greek love poet, Sappho, saying that,

> The Greek word eros denotes 'want,' 'lack,' 'desire for that which is missing.' The lover wants what he does not have. It is by definition impossible for him to have what he wants if, as soon as it is had, it is no longer wanting.[2]

I am not sure about this. I still can feel desire when feeling a connection with that which I desire. I breathe in the rose's scent and feel both filled and satisfied by it, and also open to and desiring more. This doesn't feel like lack or dissatisfaction, and certainly not like, "Oh well, I've had that. Now what?" The scent and touch of the lover's skin is like this. Desire isn't just there before one smells and touches – in the imagined contact – but also there within the contact itself, as a lingering beauty of some sort – contact firing continued desire – a paradoxical mixture of 'never enough' and 'totally enough' which can have a flavour of ecstasy about it. There is a beauty in the very availability of an erotic other. All that is needed, at any one moment, is to choose to open to it. Some Buddhist thinkers actually challenge this locking together of desire and lack. I will look more closely at these later, but I want to flag up that lack and longing might not be all there is to desire. Far too much of my life has been dominated by longing, from childhood right through most of my adult life. Often, I've not even been sure of what I am longing for – just feeling the pain and thought that something was deeply missing in my life. Finally, I got angry. I reached a point where I had had enough of it.

Longing is Not Desire

Longing is knowing
I will never have –
can't have – shouldn't have.
Longing is tinted with lack
and veined with loss.
Longing and fear of loss
imprison desire.
But I am getting old –
time thins before me.
A passionate woman is
feared by men –
distrusted by women.
Trust me or move aside
because I have a passion for life.
My love is not your longing.
My love is not what you long for.
I desire more than your love –

sweet as it is.
I want to touch and be touched
by everything.

I worked for many years with multiply disabled visually impaired young people at a special school. I learned about the importance and intricacies of touch from them and from Mike McLinden at the University of Birmingham's Department of Education. He describes at the start of his book on touch[3] how, if asked what sense they would least like to lose, many people often say sight not realising that, without touch, their lives would become meaningless. Touch is the first sense that develops *in utero* and it is often the one that is last responded to by the dying. More than any other sense it gives us information about ourselves and our environment. Touch and our constant responsiveness to it gives us our sense of vitality – of being alive. What strikes me about touch is how essential it is and yet how ambivalent we can be about it. Some of the sensory impaired young people I worked with were deaf-blind and touch was their only way to connect with and learn about the world – yet they could be very resistant to it because it was so often out of their control. Many of us can feel starved of human touch, and yet also be very averse to it. Some of this is cultural, but often it is due to early experiences of coercive or overwhelming touch. There is a huge need for touch in infants and children which, if denied or abused, will impact on later experiences of erotic desire. Woundings or repressions in our experience of touch create difficulties in accessing desire. There is also the multiplicity of meanings of the word touch – we can touch and be touched without any physical contact.

In his beautiful film, *Wings of Desire*[4], the German film maker Wim Wenders tells the story of an angel who gives up his immortality out of a desire for love through physical human touch. The passionate desire to touch that which is perceived as 'other' is known as eros, or erotic desire. When I wrote the above poem, its statement of eros seemed a ridiculously big demand, but it also felt genuine and deeply important. I would only discover later where it would lead me. Of course, there had been a long process of experience and learning to get to this point. Over many years I had to slowly realise that I was not going to fill the hole of longing with food, or a home, or an occupation, or social recognition, or with my relationship with another person. Yet I deeply wanted my desire. The anger partly came from the sense that the culture I live in conspires to keep me trapped in some sense of lack and longing. That is what creates consumerism as well as our fear and envy of others. I also feel that women are particularly culturally condemned when it comes to desire, but I will look more at that later on. Suffice it to say here that I am looking for desire that is not defined and constricted by lack, longing or loss – even though much of theory, history, literature and art seem to say it is.

BUDDHISM AND DESIRE

The Eros of reality begins with touch. There is no life without contact.
Without touch there is no desire, no fulfilment – and no mind.[1]

Contact is fundamental. In Buddhism they speak of "sense contact" as the primary experience that can lead to desire in terms of craving, clinging, attachment and aversion – all of which result in the kind of suffering Buddhists call *dukkha*, sometimes translated as unsatisfactoriness. Sense contact, in itself, is not a problem – that just happens by being alive. The problems come with what the mind can do with it.

Nature has designed living beings to move towards what is pleasant and move away from what is unpleasant. This is necessary at the base level for survival and, in itself, there is not a big problem in it – except you find you cannot simply do it. Life is hugely complex, full of obstacles to our desire for our existence to be pleasant. Even simple organisms cannot escape their own demise. Don't assume sensory pleasures will always be comfortable either. If we eat too much lovely food our stomach hurts. If we attach to a lover, it pains to part. The beautiful rose blossom we admire so much soon falls apart and drops to the muddy ground. The things we want – desire – will often become uncomfortable at times. I want to meditate. I have a strong desire to do so. It could be said that I really love it, but for many years it gave me back pain and sometimes it still causes my knees to hurt. Many of the things in life which I have truly desired and deeply loved, my children for instance, have caused me great heartache at times.

Some unpleasant experiences need to be gone through. The task is to be with them rather than turn away and close off from them. This is not easy. It's a kind of swimming against the tide and is why there is such a strong emphasis on practice in Buddhism. You need to practise – lots – with the small, everyday unpleasant things, so that you can stand a chance of being able to open to and embrace the big unpleasant things, like dying. The reward for being able to do this is peace of mind and joy – for some, this can be very deep indeed.

Change is the only thing you can count on. If you embrace impermanence, there can be a great deal of joy – even, and sometimes especially, in the changing itself. Each changing has its own pace and is in consort with every other change connected to it. If you resist the changing – and its pace – that is what the Buddhists call clinging (*upadana*) – trying to hold on to what cannot last. It creates an overall sense of *dukkha* – and *dukkha* is distinctly unpleasant. I heard the Buddhist scholar and teacher, John Peacock, once describe it as "like slowly rubbing your arm against a brick wall"[2]. That really spoke to me. *Dukkha* also happens when desire becomes craving (*tanha*) – a sense of constriction around the experience of wanting and not wanting – an inner pressure to grasp at or push away. Instead of opening to and relaxing with what is, there comes a closing and tightening, leading to all kinds of tortuous mental and emotional activity, which can feel very visceral indeed.

You would think that, because of the ultimately unpleasant result of craving and clinging, we would not indulge in them as we do. But our minds are restless, always seeking to grasp the pleasant, however we view this, and push away the unpleasant. Nothing is ever quite right, at least not for long. It always becomes 'unsatisfactory'. *Dukkha* is often defined as a sense of unsatisfactoriness, and it is. But this gives no sense of how deeply unpleasant it can make our minds and lives feel. It is not that the Buddha said that all desire is bad. There are good desires, the desire to meditate being one of them. A good desire is generally defined as one that leads towards less suffering, but we can turn even good desires into craving and clinging, and thus experience *dukkha*. We can easily feel our meditation is 'not good enough' or be disappointed when we can't reproduce a particularly lovely feeling we experienced in our last meditation. If a good desire is worked well with – through opening, relaxing, attending to it compassionately – it leads eventually to less suffering and more joy. The Buddha's Eightfold Path points to how to do this.

This is only scratching the surface of Buddhist practice and philosophy – but it is enough to see that there is certainly a lot of craving in many desires. My question here is this: Is it possible to desire without craving? If so, what does that feel like?

During my enquiry into fear, I read David Loy's book, *Lack and Transcendence*[3], and enjoyed his challenge to the assumption of lack as intrinsically necessary to our experience. He suggests that the problem of lack, and the craving it brings, arises with our concrete interpretation of self and object/other – dualism. He promotes the Buddhist view of *sunyata*, often translated as Emptiness, to alleviate the anxiety caused by the separation of self and other.

Emptiness, *sunyata*, which needs to be realised experientially to be truly integrated, is a deep knowing that all that we experience as reality is dependent on the ways in which we are perceiving it. We create our experiences of ourselves and the world – they are not other than our perception of them. We fabricate our sense of being a self, separate from the objects and others around us. This seems similar to the phenomenological idea of intentionality, which says we create 'things' and then relate to them. They exist because we experience them, and they also don't exist (as we perceive them) because there are endless different ways of perceiving them. When we deeply know the emptiness of what we desire, we can still experience and enjoy desire, but without the craving and clinging that the Buddha showed brings so much suffering into our world. It opens up more relaxed, playful, creative possibilities to our experience of being alive. This attempt to describe *sunyata* is, I acknowledge, limited by my current understanding. But even this much understanding really helps me with my experience of desire as something I can open to rather than suffer from.

Within Tibetan Buddhism, there is a Tantric tradition of using desire as a means of psychological and spiritual transformation. The whole of this tradition and the practices within it are based on *sunyata*. To make this even clearer, they use the imaginal – elaborate visual, sometimes sexual images created within the imagination and related to through an embodied desire. They are fabricated – not real – but they have profound effects on the practitioner's experience of themselves, their lives and the whole world around them.

> *Tantra is the unfolding of a creative process which occurs moment by moment in the act of manifestation and transformation. In this sense we continually experience the process of creative transformation in every aspect of our life. When the process unfolds naturally as an expression of our true nature we experience a flow of vitality in all we do...* [4]

I have had only a limited experience of these Tibetan practices, so cannot personally attest to their effect on my experience of desire. My imaginal world is more kinaesthetic than visual, and these practices rely strongly on visual imagery, so I found them difficult to enter into fully. But I can see how they might be very powerful within the freedom that *sunyata* (Emptiness) offers.

Mark Epstein, a psychiatrist and Buddhist practitioner, agrees with the potential of opening up to and including desire, promoting the role of desire in a full and meaningful life, including in Buddhist practice. His suggestion is to "make desire into a meditation" and gives helpful examples. He still maintains that desire "springs from a place of incompleteness" and describes the same, now familiar, process of turning our perceptions into things as being what sets us up for the *dukkha* of desire. Epstein promotes what he calls a "feminine" view of desire.

> *This feminine desire is not for penetration but for space. The space that is longed for is not just a space within, as a concrete equation with the vagina might lead one to suspect, but is for a space that is also without: a space between individuals that makes room for the individuality of both parties and for meeting at the edge.*[5]

This resonates with the Javanese Buddhist movement artist and teacher, Suprapto Suryodarmo's emphasis on having a "clear, empty axis" and on "dialogue" in his Joged Amerta movement practice. Prapto, as he is known by his students, was a Buddhist and this deeply informed his life and his teaching. I was able to periodically participate in movement workshops with him for eight years, including a month spent with him in Java in 2013. It was there that I began trying to understand what he meant by "clear, empty axis", but it took a full eight years to gradually experience it in my own body – "slowly, slowly" as Prapto would say – "relaxed, empty axis starts from having space inside".[6] It is difficult to put the experience into words, but it has a huge impact on my movement, on my life and my experience of what I want in life. For me, it is a multi-level experience, physical, emotional, energetic and psychic – a sense of opening up space inside and also space between myself and the environment. It requires me to become aware of and let go of the craving kind of desire – and the tendency to project these desires onto the other, where they become objectified and seen only through the lens of my desire. Only then can there be the possibility of real dialogue between oneself and the other – whether that is a person, a tree or a whole audience. The tendency to project our desires onto the other means we cannot really see or experience the other as they are – and will not be making a real connection with them. In my first experience of this teaching in a workshop with Prapto, he asked us to move with a chair.

> *Object not only object, also subject. They have their own being. Not only to use. Respecting it. Working with the subject of the object. Chair as Bodhisattva – offering itself.[7]*

This way of perceiving was a huge shift for me. Later that evening he talked in a similar way about the traditional Javanese way of viewing nature.

> *All nature is a being – alive, sacred and family – the ultimate ancestor. We connect to the whole of life from the common field of home. The sacred is not separate from the home and the family. Things are beings.[8]*

In terms of impulse (the sense of *I want to move here* or *in this way*) Prapto always recommended us to "ride it rather than be taken for a ride by it". This, of course, relies on one being aware of the impulse and understanding that we have *choice* – and he helped us practise that by getting us to "stop – relax – feel the form – open up the space" – and only then, continue with our movement. A main factor in how Buddhist meditation enables greater awareness is that it slows everything down. Joged Amerta takes this slower approach to movement and to life.

Prapto, like Epstein, spoke of finding a more feminine approach to desire. He was fond of telling the Hindu story of Uma and Shiva, as it is told in the Javanese Wayang shadow puppet theatre. In the story, Shiva becomes *lost in desire* and forces himself on Uma, who has asked him to wait until they are in private. The result is they both then *become demonic*. He reflected once on this by saying, "The man cannot understand the meditation of the woman. Always wants penetration of the Emptiness".[9] This mirrors Epstein's statement above.

I once asked him directly about how to work with desire.

> *How to open up the space around desire? Not to deny it – control it by saying, "No!" Rather to wait more. Think and feel more prior to eating a desired food. Then eat it <u>slowly</u>![10]*

This suggestion about "opening up the space around desire" feels fundamental in terms of enabling desire to become more than simply craving and grasping.

Buddhist teacher Rob Burbea, who wrote an extraordinary guide to Emptiness practices[11], maintains that: "Desire can come from a place of sufficiency. It doesn't need to come from lack."[12] According to him, always turning to the sense of lack in desire can be a habit, and connected to a wounding in our past. It is possible to see desire differently. Desire can be experienced as visceral, energetic, emotional, sexual and even spiritual – but it entirely rests on the imagination and on Emptiness. It is fabricated, created out of the separation of self from other, but becomes a felt experience. Buddhist meditation practice, by slowing our experience down and sharpening our awareness, helps us see this fabrication in action and how our mind can produce seemingly endless ruminations around our desires, creating ever more craving. Once uncoupled from craving and clinging, desire is simply for *more* of a perceived desired other, and what we most deeply desire is actually available – because we create it. It is this understanding that enables Tantric practitioners to use desire as a transformational vehicle.

It is interesting to me that the sense of space, or spaciousness, described by Epstein, is present in the Emptiness practices in Rob Burbea's book. From him I have learnt that an inner experience of constriction, a tightening in the body, heart or mind, is a sign that some kind of craving or clinging is present. Remembering to open up a sense of space inside seems to immediately bring greater ease and well-being to my experience. When I meditate on desire, as Burbea and Epstein suggest, I can open up space inside whenever I notice I am tightening around some associated feeling or thought. This is sensed in the 'energy body' which, in itself, is an imagined, but felt experience that has greatly facilitated my enquiry into deep desire, and led directly to my finally getting some experience of Prapto's relaxed, empty axis.

Burbea maintains that our desire can be an intrinsic element of an on-going exploration, facilitating and ever deepening a process he calls Soul-making[13]. It is, as he says, simply a way of looking. When we connect to our deep desire in our bodies and our imagination, we are able to open to it and invite more of it into our lives, without feeling any sense of lack, or reducing it to craving and clinging. This resonates with my reaching for roses. He offers a practice of desire where, if you notice some *dukkha* or some desire in yourself, and keep asking what it is you are really wanting, letting go of the object and going more deeply into the sense of wanting, opening up your body to the current of energy in the wanting – *really, really open* – a sense of aliveness and abundance can arise – "a feeling that what I really wanted is here – already available".[14] It is a radical approach to desire, and does not sit comfortably with everyone in the Buddhist community, but many who have tried it, myself included, find it freeing, playful and deeply meaningful.

GRECO-ROMAN VIEWS OF DESIRE

Many of our western cultural concepts, attitudes and frameworks for regarding and interpreting our experience have historical roots in the Greco-Roman world – ideas about values, both aesthetic and ethical, and about enquiry itself, and also about desire. Here I want to look at those ideas that have impressed themselves on me and my experience of desire.

Greek mythology is deeply embedded in western culture, passed on to us by the European Renaissance in particular. This can be seen in our education, art and literature, including children's stories. If we were to take the stories of the Greek immortals as evidence of how people in ancient Greece lived, it would give us a view of them living highly desire-fuelled lives. Once a Greek god or goddess desired something, which mythology indicates they did a lot, then they found a way to obtain it, often by force or trickery. But we have other sources in literature and philosophy that temper this view.

Eros, the god of love and sexual passion, was a trickster. Anyone struck by an arrow from his bow, was consumed by overwhelming desire for whoever they set eyes upon. Centuries later, Shakespeare used this motif in his play, *A Midsummer Night's Dream*, where Puck creates havoc with some "love juice" given to him by Oberon, King of the Fairies. Not only does he cause Titania, Queen of the Fairies, to fall in love with an ass-headed simpleton, but he re-directs the desire in true lovers, causing hurt and confusion. There are direct references within the play to Cupid (Eros) and his bow. Two stories about Eros that have personally affected me are 'Eros and Psyche' and the very different story of 'Daphne and Apollo'.

'Eros and Psyche' comes to us, in the form we know, from the Roman writer, Apuleius[1], but it is thought to be a much older story. In it, Psyche, a beautiful young woman, is sacrificed by her father, the king, to save the kingdom from the wrath of Venus (Aphrodite) who is jealous of her beauty. She is set up on a high crag to be the 'bride' of a dragon who would certainly devour her. But Psyche does not die, she is instead whisked off by the West Wind and taken to a beautiful palace. There, although she is alone in the daytime with all her physical needs more than met, at night, in the dark, someone comes and lays down beside her – and makes her very happy indeed. She does not know this, but her new lover/husband is Eros, son of Venus, who had fallen in love with her and saved her from death. At night, when Eros comes, she can talk with him and touch him but cannot see him. In the day she is lonely without human companionship. Eros tells her that her sisters are grieving for her and she is distraught that she can bring them no comfort. Eventually, she persuades her husband to let her meet with her sisters, and they put into her head the idea that she must be married to a monster, and that she should light a lamp when he is asleep and slay him. Of course, when she does light the lamp, who should she see but the gorgeous Eros. A drop of hot oil from the lamp lands on Eros and burns him, waking him up. He immediately tells her that now he must leave her and flies away. The rest of the story is about her journey to find him again. The gods and goddesses cannot help her because of their ties to Venus, and Venus abuses her and sets her impossible tasks. Help is found in the natural world around her. Initially it is Pan, the goat-footed shepherd, who comforts her, and then she is helped to succeed in her tasks by such things as little ants, a reed growing in a stream, and an eagle. Finally, Venus sends her into the underworld to bring back the beauty ointment of Persephone, Queen of the Underworld. Psyche despairs and believes she must kill herself in order to go to the underworld. She climbs a high tower to throw herself off, but the tower speaks to her and tells her how she can safely go to, and return from, the land of the dead. She brings back the beauty ointment, but before going with it to Venus, she thinks she should try just a little of the ointment herself, so that Eros will not be able to resist her. The result is an immediate deathlike sleep. Eros, who has been recovering from his burn, goes in search of her. When he finds her, he wipes the ointment off, returning it to its container – then wakes her with a tiny prick from one of his arrows. He tells her to take the ointment immediately to Venus, while he goes off to his grandfather, Jove (Zeus), to beg for his help and support. This he is given, in return for enabling Jove in his own amorous quests. Psyche is made an immortal and gives birth to a daughter – called Voluptas (Pleasure).

I first read the story of Eros and Psyche as a child – not in this form, but in a fairy tale. There are many fairy and folk tales that have their roots in this myth, including Beauty and the Beast and The Snow Queen, but the one I knew and loved was a Scandinavian tale. When I was seven, I was given a copy of Gwyn Jones's retelling of *Scandinavian Legends and Folk-tales* that I still have and still enjoy. There are many wonderful stories in this book, but the one I loved the most was "East of the Sun and West of the Moon"[2] – an only lightly disguised version of Eros and Psyche. In this version, she is given by her father to a great White Bear in return for the family being lifted out of poverty. The White Bear is actually a prince, condemned to be a bear in the daytime by a wicked troll step-mother. I can only surmise now that there was something about the girl's aloneness, fear, resilience and constant searching for her love that meant so much to me, even as a seven year old, inspiring in me both hope and desire. She has a desire so strong that it enables her to face many daunting and difficult things – and there are forces and beings she encounters in the journey that help her along the way. It is the same in the Greek version. Psyche means soul and so, on one level, the desire is the soul's – to find passion, love and a sense of reconnection. Maureen Murdock, who wrote about the heroine's journey in contrast to the hero's journey[3], cites the story of Eros and Psyche as a template for a woman's search for herself.

I came across the myth of Daphne and Apollo as an adult – and it appalled me. The source of the story is Ovid's *Metamorphoses*[4], which has inspired writers, artists and poets for many centuries. It was probably in a painting that I first saw the image of a woman (the nymph, Daphne) turning into a laurel tree in order to escape the clutches of an overly amorous man (the god, Apollo), but I don't remember the artist. Here is desire gone badly wrong. Apollo had been arrogant and dismissive of Eros, who then shoots an arrow with the desire to possess into Apollo and another with the desire to avoid possession into Daphne. It was the fate of Daphne that affected me the most – her fear and what she needed to do in order to find safety from another's desire – to abandon her body. When her strength begins to fail her, she calls out to her father, the river god Peneus, and he turns her forever into a tree – just in time. Apollo's arm has already wrapped around her waist, as it becomes a trunk. I have since felt that my response to this image relates to my childhood experience, which I will look at later. Suffice it to say here that this myth, and the image at the end of it, encapsulates for me a deep ambivalence I have experienced around erotic desire and connection that took many years to work through.

During the time of this enquiry, I read Nora Bateson's personal response to the myth of Daphne and Apollo[5]. When she saw Bernini's 17th century marble sculpture of the pair in Rome, she found it "heartbreakingly beautiful". As a work of art I am sure it is, but it is the stories we weave around an image like this that create our own meanings.

In her retelling of the myth, there are some elements I don't recognise – like Daphne having enjoyed Apollo's attentions before the fated arrows fell – and that, once flesh touched flesh, an antidote to the poisons in Eros's arrows was meant to release – neither of which are in the version of Ovid I know. But she asks some interesting questions, particularly about what our relationship is with the natural environment we are intimately connected to. If we love it, what is that love? The desire to possess is damaging – "possession is not love". The desire to merge into nature has its own problems. Merging rules out erotic love and desire – with no sense of 'other' left. And she asks what kind of alternative mythology can be told about this relationship?

> *Is there a mythology that can release us from the grip of havingness? To adore the world around me as I would be adored, and never find the end of the strings that pull?*[6]

I feel a sensual, erotic connection is possible that does not have the tension of craving – wanting to grasp, have, possess. Bateson says that "it is an art to ache"[7] but does this bring us back to the lack in longing? I'm not sure it does. Deep connection, inner and outer, can be alive within relationship and interaction. Where there is interaction, there is a space between, and there lies desire.

Moving on from mythology to the experience of mortals, Sappho, the Greek poet of Lesbos, could be said to be an archetypal poet of desire. She turned desire, itself, into an art form back in the 7th century BCE. Her love poems are sensuous personal descriptions of an aching desire for one who is unavailable. Anne Carson, a modern translator of Sappho, maintains that, for the ancient Greeks, lack and longing were essential aspects of desire – the focus is on the inaccessibility of the one who is desired.

> *Whoever desires what is not gone? No one. The Greeks were clear on this. They invented eros to express it.*[8] *and …where eros is lack, its activation calls for three structural components – lover, beloved, and that which comes between them.*[9]

I have mentioned this view above, when discussing lack and longing, and it is noteworthy that this way of seeing desire has such a long history in our culture. Carson maintains that it comes out of burgeoning self-consciousness, the separating out of self from non-self. She says, "self forms at the edge of desire"[10], but would it not be as true to say desire forms at the edge of self? Of course, there needs to be a perception of otherness for there to be desire. There needs to be the perceiver, that which is perceived as other – and a space between. What is this space between? And does it need to be viewed as an obstacle?

Carson says the self-consciousness in Sappho's poetry was a result of the huge change that the development of literacy brought to the Greeks when the Phoenician alphabet arrived sometime in the 8th century BCE. Until then, except for the much earlier Mycenaean Linear B script that disappeared hundreds of years before this, Greek culture had been an oral culture. According to Carson, written language allowed the ancient Greeks to begin to reflect on their inner experience. She emphasises the sensory difference between having a largely aural awareness of the world and the more visual awareness that comes with reading and writing, and proposes,

> *If the presence or absence of literacy affects the way a person regards his own body, senses and self, that effect will significantly influence erotic life. It is in the poetry of those who were first exposed to a written alphabet and the demands of literacy that we encounter deliberate meditation upon the self, especially in the context of erotic desire. The singular intensity with which these poets insist on conceiving eros as lack may reflect, in some degree, that exposure.*[11]

Sometime during the century following Sappho's time, this blossoming of self-consciousness gave rise to the philosophy of the Classical period. By the time we come to Plato (5th - 4th century BCE) the Greeks are deeply into self-consciousness and to reflecting on their thoughts, actions and feelings. Greco-Roman philosophers did not seem to take the immortals, the poets, or even the heroes of Homer, as role models in the arena of desire. In fact their approach to desire was largely one of restraint – even with Epicurus (4th - 3rd century BCE), who I came across in my first year at university. My philosophy professor was a Platonist – and I think I turned to Epicurus for relief. Epicureanism has become synonymous with hedonism – but I was to discover this was not so. There is, in all of the Greek philosophers who looked at desire, a focus on the desire for the 'good'. Epicurus seems, in ways, to be remarkably modern. He was one of those philosophers who conceived of atomic particles – and he allowed women to join his school of philosophy, which was undoubtedly radical in his own time. He was also a vegetarian. In a sense, Epicurus's views of the 'good' were not dissimilar to the Buddha's – peace of mind and freedom from fear and suffering. But his assessment of desire is largely that of drives and appetite, of which there can be natural, necessary desires which need to be simply satisfied, and unnatural, unnecessary and excessive desires which are to be avoided. His turning his attention to things like friendship, which he hugely valued, led me to presume his deep desires were for connection and positive interaction with his fellow beings. He also, obviously, liked using his mind to observe and enquire. I can relate to all of this and they are things I desire – but, at least in what are left of his works, there feels to me to be a lack of passion. Passion is generally not regarded as positive or useful by the ancient Greek philosophers, except possibly the passion for ideas.

It is the passion for the mind – the love of philosophy itself – that inspired Plato and his beloved mentor, Socrates. Plato's interesting and accessible treatise on desire is called *The Symposium*[12], after the name for a kind of evening party including food and drink. It is a male preserve and, while it could involve music and other kinds of entertainment, this one involves each guest giving an impromptu after dinner speech 'in praise of Eros', the god of Love and Desire. Socrates is present and speaks last, that is, last before the genuinely funny speech at the end 'in praise of Socrates' given by the drunken gate-crasher, Alcibiades. The focus of the speeches is mostly on the homo-erotic relationship between a man and his adolescent 'boyfriend'. It appears that, in Classical Athens, a man (the lover) could, and often did, take to his bed an adolescent boy (the loved one) who granted sexual favours in return for ethical education and, I presume, social advancement. It is clear is that this was considered normal and it is also apparent that these relationships of desire did not always have sufficient emphasis on the ethical needs, or the 'good', of the loved one. When they didn't, they were merely Common, but when they did, they were Heavenly – the epitome of Eros.

What interests me in this is the coupling of virtue and the erotic – which probably was why this treatise was repressed by certain Christian authorities until the Renaissance and even after. Part of what is problematic here are the stories we tell ourselves about Eros and the erotic. We don't tell them the way the Athenians did – and yet we can understand what they are saying in these speeches. This is the way Christopher Gill in his Introduction explains Socrates's use of the erotic.

> *...Socrates relies on the fact that the Greek word **erôs** means (interpersonal) 'love' as well as 'desire' both in a narrow sense*

> *('sexual desire') and in a broad one. He argues that love is essentially relational: that is, love is always **of** something. Love is **of** something that you need and are deficient in; so love is also essentially a state of deficiency or need (this idea is more plausible if you think in terms of desire)…Love is **of** beauty (or the good)…*[13]

Socrates speech, which is his usual masterpiece of reasoning, manages to put aside the sexual act and bring the erotic desire entirely into the mental exchange between two people. There is, for Socrates, "the 'erotic' attraction of the search for truth".[14] It is this that frustrates and infuriates the drunken Alcibiades – he wants the sex. But what Socrates wants is beauty.

> *Looking now at beauty in general and not just at individual instances, he will no longer be slavishly attached to the beauty of a boy, or of any particular person at all, or of a specific practice. Instead of this low and small-minded slavery, he will be turned towards the great sea of beauty and gazing on it he'll give birth, through a boundless love of knowledge, to many beautiful and magnificent discourses and ideas.*[15]

I can feel a passion in this – a real deep desire – but one that has left the body behind. The whole of *The Symposium* has also left women behind (and, literally, sent them out of the room) although, curiously, Socrates claims to have learned all his knowledge on the subject from a woman sage called Diotima.

Another Greco-Roman philosopher who directly addresses desire is Epictetus (1st - 2nd century CE), an adherent of the Stoic school of philosophy. Epictetus was born a slave in the Roman Empire, which is interesting in itself, as he talked a lot about freedom and slavery in relation to desire in his *Discourses*[16]. His master had access to the Roman Imperial household, recognised and supported Epictetus' abilities, and eventually freed him. Philosophers were suddenly out of favour with the Emperor Domitian at that time so, for his own safety, Epictetus moved across the Adriatic and founded a school of philosophy at Nicopolis on the west coast of Greece.

Epictetus' general advice was to focus both your desire and your aversion only on whatever is within your control – only then can you be considered free. He asks, "And can you be forced by anyone to desire something against your will?"[17] This gives his student (and us) pause for thought. He talks a lot about will – of course – and the exercise of restraint. But anyone who has tried to deal with eating issues knows that will-power has its limits in the area of desire – or can work so well that it kills you.

Epictetus' advice is basically to turn the focus of your desire and your aversion away from anything not in your power to achieve. His instructions are to give your attention to what is actually possible, then restrict yourself to choice or refusal, carefully, with "discipline and detachment"[18]. Epictetus maintains that if you can do this, it will lead to a state of tranquillity.

There Are Stoics Around – *after Billy Collins*

I came downstairs this morning
to find Epictetus sitting at the table.
He smiled – tranquilly –
as I went to open the fridge.
There were no eggs on the shelf.
"You think you want eggs, don't you?"
he chuckled – then turned towards the window
to watch the birds gorging themselves
on seed I had put out the evening before.
I sat down next to him for a while
in silent companionship,
thinking about eggs and no eggs,
and watching the birds.
"So, what do we want for breakfast?"
I asked, eventually.
But he had departed,
so I poured myself a bowl of muesli.

In ways Epictetus's tranquillity sounds like the state of equanimity so valued in the practice of Buddhism where one is no longer gripped by the craving of attachment and aversion. And, as in Buddhism, it cannot actually be reached by a simple act of will, but requires deep awareness and examination of attachment (desire) and aversion. The idea of giving attention to what is in your power to achieve brings to mind the Buddhist teacher Rob Burbea's desire practice already mentioned, which suggests that the deep desires are "already available".

Epictetus is not entirely anti-desire, nor were any of the Stoics as far as I know. The Stoic approach is more what you might call common sense and sticking with the achievable that is moderate and honourable. He makes it sound simpler than I think he knows it is. He shows how there has to be a weighing up of what you desire more/most. If you feel you deeply value freedom and honour (as the Stoics tend to), the choices of turning from desires that are outside your control and engaging in "discipline and detachment" become more obvious. So you have to go down deep to feel what it is that you really want. These deep desires need to be achievable to be effective at helping to moderate all the other competing desires that can arise.

Bruno Snell, as cited by Iain McGilchrist[19], tells us that the very concept of depth as I am using it, in the sense of deep values and deep desire, was present even for an early Greek philosopher like Heraclitus (6th-5th century BCE), coming out of its use in early Greek poetry.

> *Concepts like 'deep knowledge', 'deep thinking', 'deep pondering', as well as 'deep pain' are common enough in the archaic period. In these expressions, the symbol of depth always points to the infinity of the intellectual and spiritual, which differentiates it from the physical.*[13]

Given his personal history, I wonder if the roots of Epictetus's approach might be in the desires for freedom and for having one's autonomy respected. These are deep desires which are coloured by both cultural and personal differences in their meaning. You can see these desires arising in infant development, rising again in adolescence – but then often getting lost in the competing desires/demands of adulthood, sometimes leaving people with a sense of not having really lived their own life. Epictetus must have been able to live with not being free in the ordinary sense (he had no choice while he was a slave), but he obviously deeply valued inner freedom.

The concept of democracy and freedom of the individual that arose strongly in the 18th century, particularly in France and in the nascent United States of America, had been preceded by a huge, often violent, Protestant Reformation upheaval in Europe in the 16th and 17th centuries around freedom of worship. It also coincided with the rise of neo-classical ideas that harked back to what were perceived as the ideas and values of the Greco-Roman period, including the democracy of ancient Athens. The desire for freedom has been expressed in many times and many places throughout history. That is not to say that everyone prioritises this desire. Some people place their desire for safety and security or for things to remain as they are (the status quo) before their desire for freedom. But is this just prioritising 'freedom from' (hunger, uncertainty, pain, fear etc.) over 'freedom to' (move, express themselves, explore, question, develop, etc.)? And then, of course, there is the desire for freedom from desire, in the Buddhist sense.

When I ponder deeply about the desire for freedom, I go down into my body and feel into a sense of not being free. It feels immediately tight and constricted. If I go with this further into the place of oppression, the images are of being bound, closed in, behind a barrier that I can see through but cannot open and go out – no access to the unlimited possibilities of being alive. A feeling of anger arises at being unfree. This is an anger that can lead to violence, revolt and war. It feels powerfully energetic. I want to burst the chains that bind, break down the walls and push aside, even hurt, anyone that I feel is linked to my oppression or might try to block my movement to freedom.

When oppression is there – one person or group denying the dignity and freedom of another person or group – something needs to change. How to bring about that change for all those involved – maximise both the freedom from and the freedom to – is a complex social issue that we must continue to address. But what Epictetus focused on was inner freedom – and its opposite, self-oppression. While the desire for freedom may be ubiquitous, the solutions are particular, perhaps, to the individual.

For me, the desire for freedom is a deep one. It resonates through my body and my heart. I recognise the feeling of constriction from my meditation practice – and I know that it is a sign of what in Buddhism is called craving – that particular kind of desire to grasp at, cling to or push away whatever is seen as desirable or undesirable contact. It is associated with the sense that things are not as they should be, a feeling of dissatisfaction that in Buddhism is called *dukkha*. How to transform this craving is one of the main thrusts of Buddhist teachings.

I have learned, from Buddhist meditation practices and from Qigong, a way of following my desire for freedom that is not about engaging with the constriction through anger and effort. Both anger and effort bring an even greater sense of constriction. Freedom, instead, comes through relaxing more and opening more – becoming softer and more vulnerable, but without collapsing. Initially, this feels counter-intuitive. For instance, fear triggers the desire to escape what is seen as frightening and to find safety. In a survival situation, this is essential. But if it is not a real, here-and-now survival situation, but rather some past script in the mind, the desire to escape becomes craving. The mind and body feel constricted, insisting that you escape in whatever way you have learned to in your life. I withdraw behind my inner defences and, by so doing, become less free. I may believe myself to then be freer from the source of the fear, but my 'freedom to' has been seriously compromised – and the potential for erotic desire is as well.

A reflection I have had about my desire for freedom is that I don't want to be free of everything. I want to be free within a sense of also being held or contained. It's a both/and emotional dynamic and there needs to be a balance of some kind. I can feel freer to move, to create, to express myself, if I feel held in some way. I think this is just because I am a human being, and we humans always need to feel we are in some way connected to others, or at least another. I desire a sense of inner and outer freedom and feel it most when I am also held in open, warm, relaxed connection. For me, this connection can arise when I am out in nature, in meditation practice or in relationship with others. I want both to be free and to be held, so there is a need for balance. Is the balance required in freedom a balance between 'freedom from' and 'freedom to'?

What has dipping into the Greco-Roman world given me in my looking for desire? It has raised the issue of how culture and education influence desire. There have been interesting cross-overs with Buddhism – which is cross-cultural. It also reinforces the idea that it is in the space between our inner and outer experience that desire can arise. This is a creative space, and I will look next at creativity.

THE DESIRE TO CREATE

I have a desire to create – to bring into being and give form to – some *thing*. I had the desire to create this book, to create the poems and essays in it, as an expression of my general desire to create as well as my desire to enquire and to communicate. I consider being creative a deep human desire, and somewhere in any creative act there is the desire to communicate. There are endless possible ways of being creative. We are creating in an unconscious sense all the time. The theories of phenomenology and the Buddhist teachings of Emptiness both insist we are constantly creating our world – our selves and all the things we perceive. We are creating our experience through the meanings and interpretations our mind gives those things. And our experience feeds back into further fabricating. But that is not the creativity that I am desiring – although it rests on it. Desire itself rests on it.

I don't know what it is about poetry that inflames my desire. Indeed, I don't know where my poems come from. While I can consciously create the circumstances most likely to let them happen, invite the words and images, and then consciously arrange them when they arrive, the images and even the words themselves seem to come from deeper than, or beyond, my conscious mind. Countless artists, writers, musicians and theorists have attested to this "inspiration" experience. The Greek Muses were a mythological personification of the sources of creativity, but to me it feels like it is coming out of the dark, which is also how Rebecca Solnit sees it:

> *Creation is always in the dark because you can only do the work of making by not quite knowing what you're doing, by walking into darkness, not staying in the light. Ideas emerge from edges and shadows to arrive in the light, and though that's where they may be seen by others, that's not where they're born.*[1]

To create requires desire and a willingness to open to this unknown place of inspiration. It is definitely not something one can grasp at. The desire to create is a perfect example of desire without grasping. It can feel like being on the brink of an abyss – and having to relax and let go, to trust – and then to receive what arrives. If I do grasp at some kind of outcome, it causes anxiety and so I know this is more about fear than desire, and it distracts from the process of creativity itself or even aborts it.

The desire to create makes demands on the maker. At its full strength, it can push other aspects of life to one side – relationships, daily tasks, even the need to eat at times. Rob Burbea remembers someone who came on one of his retreats saying, "We are doors for what wants to come through."[2] This image implies that we open to whatever it is. Rob has also referred to Henri Corbin's use of the image of "the angel out ahead".[3] We think and feel we are forging our own path when, in fact, we have been following an angel all the time. So, is our desire to create even our desire? Can we claim ownership of it? Or are we just able, at times, to open to the desire of creation itself? Or to the angel out ahead?

There was a movement in 20th-century psychology to place the locus of our desire, including creative desire, in the space between mother and infant. D.W. Winnicott's theory of what he termed the 'transitional space' was one of the cornerstones of my training as a dramatherapist. It is here, in this space between, that the infant can first create an object other than mother. A transitional object, like a teddy or piece of cloth, can be given meaning and become something to relate to and gain comfort from.

> *Transitional objects and transitional phenomena belong to the realm of illusion which is at the basis of initiation of experience. This early stage in development is made possible by the mother's special capacity for making adaptation to the needs of her infant, thus allowing the infant the illusion that what the infant creates really exists.*[4]

Here, Winnicott says, lies the space between self and other that allows us to begin to imagine, play and create – and it is the infant's desire for contact with mother that stimulates it all. It is an erotic desire, and he says that the transitional object stands for the breast, what he calls "the object of the first relationship". I acknowledge that, for breastfed babies, the breast is a highly important object of sensory and emotional experience, but are the face, hands, arms, smell, sound and whole body of the mother/caregiver just substitutes for the breast? I love breasts – my own, my mother's, everyone's! But, to focus the origin of creative desire on the maternal breast feels somehow like colluding with a masculine sexual fetish. I also don't actually know if this whole theory of transitional object holds water outside our own culture. That's an enquiry in itself.

It does make sense to me that the initial experience of desire, as I have expressed earlier, might lie in the infant's instinctive desire/need for re-connection with the mother. Winnicott maintains that the desire to play and create requires trust – initially provided by the trust within the infant-caregiver relationship and the caregiver's ability to adapt to the infant's needs. But that doesn't mean that someone for whom this relationship has been compromised or even abusive cannot play or create – as the many neglected and abused children who have been able to make use of dramatherapy and play therapy demonstrate. With these children, the therapist will try to create a space of sufficient trust within which the child can play and create. The idea that play and creativity are inherently healing is at the foundation of these therapies, as is the importance of being with the child in the experience of play, rather than being a disinterested observer.[5]

Winnicott's description of play, a basic element of the creative process, involves the erotic, with its sensuality, bodily arousal, excitement, pleasure – and he even uses the term 'climax'. Play, he maintains, is where children can be free to create – a place of imagination, where they can learn about themselves in relation to their physical and social environments. It is in playing, he says, that the child finds their sense of self – their sense of being – and play requires the same conditions as creativity. For the desire to create to manifest there needs to be a space – a play space, let's call it. This play space is partly inner and partly outer. It is a mind-set, but also has contextual boundaries of time and environment. There is material to manipulate – play with. For the poet this takes the form of images and words. There is attention and curiosity. There is imagination. There is a constant interweaving of the subjective and objective, of inner and outer experience. And there is an opening to something not quite known. Though there may be hopes of an outcome built from knowledge, repetition and skill, the outcome in play is always different and sometimes requires a real sense of risk – of pushing limits. Both play and creativity have the frisson of desire and risk, and they involve imagination.

The imagination, an important element in desire, is essential to play and creativity. Stephen Levine puts it like this:

> *Imagination…is always embodied thinking. It carries a thought within an image, a thought which cannot be detached from the image without losing its vitality…To be alive means to be in the world as embodied beings, capable of imaging ourselves more deeply, i.e. seeing our authentic possibilities in the course of our*

> *lives...Imagination can be said to be on the 'bridge' between self and world...*[6]

Here we are again at the space between self and other/object – the place of desire and eros. Levine actually defines healing (in the arts therapies sense) as "the restoration of a person's imaginative capacity"[7]. Something I have experienced over and over with imagination – so often that I completely trust it – is that using the imagination can significantly alter my embodied experience. Our imagination frees us to change, alter, see and experience things differently – and this is effected in the body as well as in the mind. Imaginatively putting myself in a different place or a different role alters my perspective and can change my whole sense of being. This is essentially how dramatherapy works. In both Alexander Technique and in Qigong I have learned I can literally move muscles and open spaces between joints using the imagination alone. Sexual erotica is the imagination stimulating our sexual desire. All of this feels highly creative.

Another 20th-century psychoanalyst, Jacques Lacan, wrote a great deal about desire. He is known for claiming that all "desire is the desire for recognition".[8] Like Winnicott, Lacan is referring to the mother/child relationship. A conclusion like this, however elaborated on, feels to me essentially reductionist. It is reducing meaning entirely down to early experience, and a highly interpreted meaning and experience at that. And yet, I can feel some resonance with it in terms of creativity. Yes...I do desire my creativity to be recognised – and it was, most probably, my mother I wanted recognition from in my early experiences of creativity. As I grew up, my desire for recognition from my father came more to the fore. To some extent this desire for recognition of my creativity from my parents continued through my whole life – and has been transferred to others, including imagined others. I wanted my parents' love – and I loved them. I also wanted them to acknowledge me as a creative being. But does the desire to create arise in order to obtain that recognition? There is love in the mix of this desire and in this relationship. When does the desire to be loved become the desire to create? To love? Can these be separated? Remember, the Greeks used the word eros to mean both love and desire. Is the desire for recognition really the deepest desire in creativity?

The desire to create is the desire to give form – to what? What is motivating that desire? I talked with someone I know, who makes lovely things, about her desire to create.[9] She gathers all kinds of bits and pieces, then brings them together, re-forms and re-arranges them into completely unique and beautiful objects. She definitely speaks of her motivation to create in the emotional, sensual, arousal language of desire: "I can feel my heart getting excited…In the making, the working with the materials, there's something loving about it, emotional, poignant. If the desire (to create) was a colour, it's red. Feisty. Passionate. Once it arises, there's a need to move with it. It's physical." She speaks also about the desire for recognition of some kind: (What I make) "expresses who I am – a way of being seen". And she feels that sense of letting go into the unknown: "It starts with a seed of an idea, but I never know where it is going … It can be quite chaotic … I'm normally an organised person." She speaks of the desire for beauty in her desire to create: "Beauty in the obscure – in the imperfection – the weird and the wacky." She also speaks about something I have not yet mentioned – the desire to leave something behind that will exist beyond death: (I want to create) "something that is physical – that is left-over … leaving something in the world of me". I can recognise both of these last two in my own desire to create – a desire to create something of some beauty and leaving something of myself behind when I go, even if just for those who knew and loved me. The connection between beauty and creativity is seen in the Greek word for making – *poiesis* – and the ideas around it in Greek culture – that creating something beautiful can mitigate our sense of mortality.[10]

What I hope for in creating my poems is to touch another – the reader – in whatever way they happen to receive that touch. But the reader is not the object of desire for me. The poem, itself, is the object of desire. The poet Denise Levertov explains this in her own way. For her, this desire is a need.

> *This need is the need for a **poem**; when this fact is not recognized, other needs – such as an undifferentiated need for self-expression, which could just as well find satisfaction in a gesture or an action; or the need to reassure the ego by writing something that will impress others – are apt to be mistaken for specific poem-need.*[11]

My desire is fuelled by love – a deep love of language and the way language can surprise and delight me, bringing something unexpected into being. So it is for Levertov, who puts it concisely:

> *…the poet's love of language must, if language is to reward him with unlooked-for miracles, that is, with poetry, amount to a passion. The passion for things of the world and the passion for naming them must be in him indistinguishable.*[12]

Naming is at the heart of language and infants are enthusiastic about it. Naming locates and separates out. It invites associations, images, feelings and connections. Names are magical – even the most simple ones. For me, naming isn't about boxing in or defining, which is limiting and alienating. Naming creates a magical space around something or someone that can allow perception to deepen and become playful. Our minds want to name – but so do our hearts. There is a pleasure and some kind of desire expressed in naming. It creates 'the other' that we can then try to know, despite them being always intrinsically unknowable. There is something erotic about naming. That is how I have viewed the naming of birds.

Using a book, I have named flowers in hedges, fields and woods – always experiencing the pleasure of naming. But flowers want to be seen – they are dressed for it – and they stay still. Birds have always moved my heart – even without being able to name them – and I have felt a ridiculous thrill whenever I have been able to name one. For the most part, they do not want to be seen by the likes of us, and only want to be heard by us to tell us to go away. Their colours, songs and calls are for others of their own kind. I have found books of limited use in naming birds. To name, you have to know where to find them first, know what details to observe and then get them to show themselves enough to observe those details. Naming by ear is a wonderful skill that hugely increases the naming possibilities when out walking, but is not learned from books. I can identify a few birds by sound – the ones that are most present in my immediate environment: house sparrow, wood pigeon, swift, magpie, crow, blackbird, buzzard. But there are even sounds that some of these birds make that I can't distinguish. You have to repeatedly put the sound and the sight together. Best to have a teacher and guide. For me, that was Nigel.

Nigel always insisted you have to earn your birds. His ability to name birds by sight and by sound outstrips that of anyone else I have personally known. He is definitely not interested in naming as simply a way to define, and thereby limit, anything. I feel he appreciates the mystery, the undiscovered and undiscoverable of everything in nature – while still being insatiably curious. This made him my perfect teacher.

Early on, Nigel taught me to 'jigsaw' – to try to name a bird by the flying silhouette against the sky, part of what is referred to as 'jizz' in the birding world. This opened me up to the sheer beauty of bird shapes in the sky – how they fit there just so. I realised I already knew some basic jigsaws, mostly the same birds whose sounds I knew, and I began to take more interest in the aerial shapes around me. I was very pleased with this growing ability, a part of the pleasure in naming. Then I stayed in a campsite south of London and saw a shape in the sky heading for a very tall tree – a shape I had *never* seen before. I busily jigsawed away. Was it a pheasant? No, flying too high – wrong shape. Was it a corvid? Definitely not. It was only when I heard it that the penny slowly dropped. I had seen my first parakeet in the British skyscape! Pleasure is too tame a word for my feeling at this naming. I would like to remember and celebrate just a few of the naming experiences that Nigel has enabled for me.

Naming With Nigel

Dipper disappearing under a bridge –
later bouncing on a boulder in the River Teign.
Fieldfares in a field (where else!).
Many Brent Geese on a sand bar.
Red Kite infiltrating the Dartmoor sky.
Siskins whispering in woods.
A pair of Shoveler Ducks sieving at the edge of a lake.
Ring Ousel on a granite gatepost.
Crossbills, like flames flickering
on the top of tall pines.
Reed warblers repeating themselves in reeds.
Meadow Pipits undulating across the moor.
Oystercatchers and Greenshanks in shallow estuary mud.
Cattle Egrets strolling through a water meadow.
Wrens shouting their songs out from bushes and hedges.

I grow more confident in my naming.
Here are some I have done on my own:
A Chiffchaff chiffchaffing on a hawthorn tree
just a few feet above where I am lying
in the grass on a Dorset hillside.
A flock of glittering Goldfinches surfing the treetops.
A Great Black-backed Gull gliding below my eye line
as I stand on a cliff over the sea, awed by its wingspan.
A pair of Ravens pulling worms in a field before flying
into the woods, gronking to each other as they go.

A Garden Warbler singing every day from a telephone line
stretching across a midsummer garden.
Curlews calling in the black and pink dusk at Topsham estuary.
A Kingfisher dancing above the Thames near Reading (my
    first ever!)
Swifts, Swifts, Swifts and more Swifts, swooping
through my garden and over the neighbours' houses!
I know them so well yet can't even imagine what they really are –
and always I call out "Hello Swifts!" to them.
Naming in this way is not just a pleasure.
It is ecstatic!

There is inspiration – and naming seems a part of this inspiration process, at least for me as a poet and writer. Then there is the hard work of crafting, making, bringing into form. The French screenwriter Céline Sciamma has some interesting things to say about the crafting of her 2019 film, *Portrait of a Lady on Fire*.[13] She acknowledges that inspiration is "a thrilling sensation" but insists that "writing is about having desires for ideas and includes the need to build an architecture of multiple desires". Creating structure from inspiration is the task. It is "an opportunity to work on your desires rather than acting immediately on them". Writing requires "being radical with yourself – not self-indulgent at all". It requires "resisting easy pleasures and resisting the temptation of belonging". You have to go out on a limb – take a risk – a leap into something new. Listening to her took me right back to my initial desire to enquire into desire. The work, Sciamma says, lies in "getting accurate about what you want" – identifying and locating your desires for your creation. In creating a film, there are scenes that she really wants to include, and then there are scenes that seem to be needed for the story. Those scenes that seem to be needed must become desired. "You have to want every scene very deeply. It is about caring. You have to care about every detail." Anything she initially identified as needed, if she cannot turn it into a desire, she gets rid of. This gives her film a very poetic quality. It is how I see the hard work of turning an inspiration into a poem that fulfils my poem-desire. Every detail must be what I want it to be. It is only then that my desire to create feels like it has become a work of the soul. The chapters in this book are my scenes – where I care about and desire every detail. Desire is hard work.

LOOKING FOR DESIRE – SOME CONCLUSIONS

I have been looking for desire in lots of places and discovered there are many ways to view it. I have learned what I think it is not. The desire that I am looking for is not craving, grasping or wanting to possess; neither is it endless lack and longing. I would not want to desire or be desired in any of these ways. Desire does seem more feminine, as Epstein suggests – an opening to passion and beauty and a receptivity to otherness – a sense of being filled with something that enhances your life, bringing greater vitality. This may be another person, but doesn't have to be. It can be a rose or a vision of an angel. Desire stimulates and motivates – and it touches the heart. I am reminded of John Denver's 'Annie's Song', where he sings not of wanting to possess his desired other, but of her ability to "fill up my senses", following this with a wonderful list of similes from his experiences in the natural world. He then asks permission from her to allow his desire for her – which I see as a way of inviting her desire. There is great tenderness in this, care and respect, the inclusion of consent as well as adoration and desire – and the connecting of desire with the aliveness of the natural world opens up a sacred aspect in it for me. It goes down deep into the soul.

I am not looking to merge in the experience of desire either. The 'oneness' experience, while it brings its own beauty and a relief in letting go of the sense of self and other, is a different experience from desire. If this is what you desire, you will lose desire as soon as you experience merging. But, if you understand the connection between otherness and desire, allowing that you will not ever completely know the other, both desire and the other remain available to open to. When there is this sense of availability and receptivity, there comes more and more opening. Without it, there is a tightening into lack.

Desire is an outflowing of the imagination. Understanding its imaginal quality is what makes it ever possible – the imagination allows desire and its "filling up of the senses" to occur whenever you open to it. When you bring this understanding into the material realm and the physical touching is tender, the other, be that a person or a rose, will be allowed their otherness – desire will be alive and the contact open, in the imagination and in the physical touching. Both love and desire grow with understanding and allowing the otherness of the loved one – and opening to them.

I first heard 'Annie's Song' as a young adult, and it deeply moved me. It seemed to encapsulate what I was looking for in a relationship, but had not found. It suggests that desire, love and the "filling up of senses" with another person was possible – filled with the beauty of the kinds of natural experiences that I well understood and loved. For me, the problem has been with opening to the human other. To truly touch desire, that opening was necessary.

GROWING THROUGH DESIRE

Tell me, what is it you plan to do
with your one wild and precious life?

Mary Oliver, 'The Summer Day'

WOMEN AND DESIRE

How can I approach the vast subject of women and desire? How can I do it justice? How can I honour all women, now and down through the ages, in their desire? I can't – I can only share my own particular experience. Looking at deep desire through the lens of being a woman necessitates looking at my own journey of becoming a woman and encountering the many desires that arose within it. I knew it was, somehow, at the heart of my enquiry but suddenly felt unsure how to approach it, fearful even – and then I was called away by the needs of others and by my concern for them. This is what happens so often to women. Why? The more I sat with these questions, the more I became aware of some kind of energy coming up. I began to become 'big' – too big, as others in the past have told me. I was loud and emphatic when talking. I wanted to shout sometimes for apparently no reason. Of course, it didn't take me long to recognise that I was angry. Although I knew it was related to women's desires, I was not clear about the anger and I didn't want it to hurt those close to me. I tried to say that it was not about them, but anger energy triggers fear in others and I felt I had to rein it in and try to sift through it from a distance rather than embody it. I felt resentful about having to do this – yet again. The sense of somehow being too much for others to cope with, if I really come out and be myself, is an old feeling – one that I resent but have not known how to get past. Luckily, I have some women friends who understand what this is like – because they too live with the frustration of it.

In order to re-orientate myself within women and desire I went back to read Audre Lourde whose wonderful essay, *Uses of the Erotic: The Erotic as Power*,[1] had resonated deeply with me when I first read it. But this time I went to an essay where she looks at anger. I found exactly the same dilemma – and Lourde's refusal to collude with it. Her poetry and writing is full of tenderness, pain and eroticism. She is also articulate about her anger and about her struggle to work effectively with it.

> *My fear of anger taught me nothing. Your fear of that anger will teach you nothing, also…I have used learning to express anger for my growth.*[2]

Her willingness to identify herself as a black lesbian feminist in the 1970s opened her to attack from all directions, from men and women, black men and black women included – and from the mainly white feminists of this period.

> *I speak out of direct and particular anger at an academic conference, and a white woman says, 'Tell me how you feel but don't say it too harshly or I cannot hear you.' But is it my manner that keeps her from hearing, or the threat that her life might change?[3]*

What must change for women to be able to embrace the fullness of their desire? And to hear the anger of having it denied?

Then a friend sent me a link to listen to Mona Eltahawy.[4] Eltahawy's experience is as a Muslim woman, born in Egypt, who has also lived in England and now in the US. Due to her parents' work, she lived in Saudi Arabia as a teenager, and it was here that she encountered the full force of patriarchal oppression. In Saudi Arabia she discovered that a woman is "the walking embodiment of sin". She was repeatedly groped when on the Hajj pilgrimage to Mecca at the age of 15. This began her radicalisation. Eltahawy is now one of the most delightfully radical feminists of the 21st century. But it has come hard to her. Feminism initially scared her, and she took to wearing the hijab because it "hides the body from all the assaults and groping". She was not able to discard it for many years. She found that "women with opinions makes them a target". In the Egyptian uprising in 2011, she was arrested by the police, beaten, had both her arms broken, was sexually assaulted and threatened with rape. She knows it was only her connections and notoriety that enabled her to be freed, rather than be raped and possibly killed. When she wanted to explore her own eroticism, she found that she scared most men. She was unable to feel desire for a man who was scared of her, so it took a while. As with Lourde, Eltahawy says that "anger fuels my work…angry women are free women". It is her stated goal for "every woman to set her own agenda". But I have found it hard to find and know what my own agenda around desire actually is.

I realised I could not look deeply into my desire as a woman without addressing my anger about my desire being distorted and defined by others, and having to repress or sublimate it. Anger is connected with fear – but it is the activating side of the fear response, designed to confront the cause of the fear. It brings enormous energy with it, which can be harnessed to enable action and change. This is part of what Audre Lourde meant in expressing anger for growth. It is also why Mona Eltahawy so enthusiastically embraces both anger and desire. I need the energy to move past the conditioning and suppression of desire in my upbringing and culture. I *want* my own desire.

Some of the anger I feel now goes back to being nine years old and finding myself the object of a grown man's desire. I did not understand what was going on – how could I? But I did know he was the first man who wanted to cuddle me, and it felt lovely – that is, until it felt confusing and finally unsafe. This took a while, because I loved him – how could I not? And I thought I was special to him. It was a slightly older girl, who had obviously also been subject to this man's desire to cuddle girls, who first made me question what was going on. She was twelve and I was ten. She asked me if I didn't think there was something strange, not quite right, about the way he kept wanting to get physically close. Shortly after this, he began trying to put his tongue in my mouth. I didn't know what it was, but I knew that was not how adults kissed children and it felt wrong somehow. Of course, all this made me question if there was something also wrong with my own desire to be physically close to another. I felt shame. I began to pull back and protect myself from his embraces. He would try to corner me alone at times, and then I would have to be quite forceful in wriggling out of his arms and getting away. He was a member of the family, and I never spoke about it to anyone or even verbally reprimanded him. I felt I was protecting him as well as myself. I had to keep us both safe – a ten-year-old girl taking responsibility for a grown man's desire. That is something to be angry about.

This directly relates to Mona Eltahawy's description of how men in Saudi Arabian culture make women responsible for men's unwillingness to take responsibility for their own desire. It just happens to them and women are the cause of it and must bear the consequences. This masculine lack of responsibility is sanctioned by patriarchy. Masculine desire is used to blame, oppress, exploit and disempower women. It is not about individual men, although they are caught up in it. It is part of the unquestioned assumption of male power and privilege within patriarchy. Children are also caught up in and damaged by the patriarchal disowning of responsibility and assumption of power and privilege. The conditions for responsible desire are missing – equality and consent.

Not only are women abused by male desire, but we are disconnected from our own. Even in the fairy tales told to children, women do not often fare well when it comes to desire. Dire consequences can result from women following their own desire, even the desire for a child as in *Prince Lindworm* or *The Wild Swans*, both stories I read as a child[5]. But the most terrible tale of what can happen to a woman who follows her desire is *The Red Shoes*[6]. All this poor orphaned girl wants is a pair of shoes – but she is mistakenly given red shoes, the colour of passion, and her love of wearing them takes her on a terrible dance of ostracism, exhaustion, mutilation and eventually death. The message is that it is both wrong and dangerous for women to entertain and follow their own desire.

We are supposed to want what others want, especially the men in our lives – only, deep down, we don't. We have our own desires. This creates confusion and men complain they don't know what women want. But patriarchy makes it almost impossible for women, themselves, to know what they want. One of the things I realised as I reflected on all this is that I not only want to be desired and to feel my own desire, I want my desire desired – the subtle tenderness of it and the full force of it. I want to be able to express my own desire and be loved and desired for it, rather than be seen as greedy, aggressive, scary or 'too much'. Audre Lourde knew that if women really connected with their own inner erotic sensibilities, they would feel hugely empowered. She writes of several ways in which the erotic can empower women, but this one spoke deeply to me.

> *Another important way in which the erotic connection functions is the open and fearless underlining of my capacity for joy. In the way my body stretches to music and opens into response, hearkening to its deepest rhythms, so every level upon which I sense also opens to the erotically satisfying experience, whether it is dancing, building a bookcase, writing a poem, examining an idea…For once we begin to feel deeply all the aspects of our lives, we begin to demand from ourselves and from our life-pursuits that they feel in accordance with that joy we know ourselves to be capable of.*[7]

This erotic knowledge of joy shakes the self-abnegation in women taken for granted in patriarchal society – and it brings together the sexual, the sensual and the spiritual in the same way a rose does.

'Dreaming Sphinx' – *a sculpture by Wendy Froud*

Kiss my neck, my darling.
Run your hands over
my shoulders and breasts.
Let my hair fall around you
in a dark, perfumed embrace.

Stay awhile – dream the dream.

Do not fear my tail
and claws! They are
for grasping the earth –
holding on to that
from which we all emerge.

Sacred loins – resting on rock.

My sense of myself, and therefore of my desire, is grounded in my early experiences of being in the world with others. I have already looked at my birth experience and resulting relationship with my mother earlier in this book, but I was born into a 1950s' nuclear family that was its own unique system. Growing up within it created complex "contextual mutual learning through interaction"[8] that needs to be understood in terms of how it affected my relationship with desire. One of the main features of it was the paucity of actual interaction.

My father was the main role model for the masculine through my early childhood. He was a brilliant rising star in his academic field of radar and radio science. I hold a lasting memory of him sitting with a yellow pad of paper on his lap, writing endless long equations – or pacing slowly from his study, across the bare pine floorboards of the downstairs hallway and into the living room, then back again, over and over as he thought things through. It was almost a heartbeat pace – soothing me into sleep at night. I have thought he was also, most probably, on the autistic spectrum. He did not do emotions – except for occasional, sudden and, to a child, overwhelming outbursts of anger. Neither I nor my siblings were cuddled or played with by either of our parents once we were out of babyhood. The most positive interactional experience I had with my father as a small child was to be read a story at bedtime. He was very good at this and, until my sister took my place, I got to sit on his lap. The household revolved around his needs and desires – patriarchy in miniature. My mother adored him and facilitated him in countless ways, not only by providing him with a beautiful, quiet and controlled home environment where he could relax and continue to do his thinking, but in creating the necessary social events an ambitious academic needs to be involved in. She was a wonderful hostess, much loved and admired by those who received her hospitality. At a gathering, all my father had to do was stand there and respond thoughtfully when anyone talked to him. But my enduring sense of my mother is that she was lonely, and my father was not able to meet her in her emotional depths. There was a deep sadness and unfulfilled desire in her that, as I put it to one therapist, I felt I drank in with her milk. Her love for and commitment to her husband and her ability to sublimate her frustrated creativity in her social and domestic activities was admirable – but she ended up an alcoholic. What was the mutual learning in this context?

We were all learning to live with emotional isolation. We each adapted to our situation in our own ways. I felt estranged from my older brothers as a child and I was a nuisance to my sister. There were no other children my age nearby and, even though she was five years younger than me, I coerced her at times into being a playmate for me. This held limited satisfaction for me, and was problematic for my sister, as she revealed to me later in life. Mostly, as I began to grow older, I became more and more solitary. My main solace and sense of connection came from the natural world around me and from books. What I most wanted was to grow up and leave. I believed, deep in my heart, that love and connection with another would be available to me as an adult, even though they were not present then in my life.

The Slaterville Road *(upstate New York)*

The long road stretches straight in both directions.
Heat ripples above melting tarmac, untouched
by the shade of front yard trees where
hidden birds rest in their mid-day torpor.

I cross over the deep ditch on a slab of slate,
pull down the flap of our post box
on top its bare wooden stake and remove
letters and a rolled up copy of the Ithaca Journal.

Intoxicated by summer's freedom,
my brother is shooting peas at passing trucks,
until a driver stops, drags him wide-eyed
up the front steps and bangs on the screen door.

Later, in bed, aching with desire to grow up soon,
I listen to the gradual approach of a lone car,
its lights bending and floating across the wall opposite,
dwindling away into the distance.

My inner desires as a child, for contact and holding, and for escape from the isolation I felt myself living in, remained as I moved into puberty and young adulthood. But new impulses arose from my developing body and they could easily take me into feelings and actual situations I might not otherwise have ventured into. Sexuality has its own motivations that bring with them powerful desires, infusing the heart and imagination, creating new, confusing and surprisingly compelling images and impulses. Nature takes no account of individual lives – so, making havoc with the life of a young girl is just fine. Fundamentally, it wants to create more life – expressing its essentially erotic nature. Watching the blackbird pulling up worms to feed the nestlings, I can see death and life are one. The overwhelming or death of any one individual being matters not if more life might result. A single sexual encounter where one person is damaged matters not from Nature's perspective, and Nature's desires are powerful. So sexual desire is risky territory for the individual. The risks for women expressing and exploring their sexual desire are particularly great: shame, ostracism, degradation, abuse, damage and even death. The risks almost always come in the form of other people, particularly, but not only, men. The role of other women in sexually oppressing women is ancient and well known.

Through adolescence I found myself moving towards and wanting to connect with others – particularly in my own peer group. I learned to quietly hold my own with them and I made a few friendships that eased the isolation experienced when I was younger. Although I found social gatherings, like parties and dances, excruciating and unsafe, I developed crushes and eventually, at the age of 17, fell in love. This is all perfectly normal.

My first love was as beautiful and safe as I could have wished for. I still cherish that relationship after over 50 years. It began a tender awakening of my sexuality – but was of greater importance in the awakening of the possibility of a deep and intimate friendship with another human being.

However, sexual passion was missing – and I sensed the lack without understanding what it was. I experienced periods of restlessness and frustration, which I didn't fully understand and couldn't really explain to my confused boyfriend. I slowly closed the doors on that intimate relationship, without initially even realising it, and this precipitated my first experience of depression. In my life I have experienced several bouts of lengthy depression – some deeper and longer than others – and desire is hard to locate in this place. I have never arrived at the point of reaching a true desire for death, but I certainly know the lack of desire for anything at all. There has always been something that keeps me going – but it never feels like desire.

My boyfriend was a good friend in that time, and I found my way through the depression with his support, and with advice from a graduate student in the History department of my university – start writing a journal, she said. I have kept journals on and off ever since – an invaluable tool for self-reflection and understanding.

My Friend – *for PF*

We were always better friends than lovers –
the best verbal intercourse I've ever known –
conversations long, deep and satisfying.
We were two children together,
playing at being grown up and in love.
The lessons on love I learned then
have lasted a lifetime –
listening, trust, tenderness, care.

I thought love was all I needed,
but my body thought otherwise.
The fire had been laid without fully igniting
and my desire made me restless.
I went halfway across the world to blaze into woman,
only to find another man-child
and become lost in the smoke and the flames.
Still, our conversations flowed in pen and ink.

Love lies between us,
as much as continent and sea –
and more than fifty years.

When I flew west one last time
to sit together, walk together, eat together
and talk again,
It was you, my friend,
I wanted to see.

The 1960s and 70s were known as a time of sexual revolution, but much of this was on the surface and included a great deal of male exploitation of women. The greatest sexual benefit it brought to women was the pill, enabling them to take contraception into their own hands. My own journey of trying to understand and express sexual desire has been a long one – initially facilitated by the pill, but also complicated by a long-lived ambivalence about physical closeness created by my childhood experiences. I was confused by the underlying cultural definitions of what sexual desire should look like. When I first opened to my own sexual desire, the quality of relationship was side-lined, though I tried hard to imagine including it.

Catalyst

Sick and shivering
and wanting more –
deserting all loyalties
but to the pulsing,
queasy body fever –
singing and shaking –
opening locks on
hot, dark doors –
pulling him along corridors
and into empty elevators –
up or down matters not –
just the rush of reaction –
girl heedlessly undoing herself –
irreversibly rearranging
her chemistry.

Careless and unconsumed,
he moves on.

Feeling myself a failure in sustaining an intimate relationship, I withdrew from any attempt to and, again, slid into depression. Despite this habit of retreat, my contradictory desire to connect was strong enough – and my curiosity about life was alive enough – to eventually lead me again into risky territory, which included the arenas of theatre and of personal development. Here, I found myself confused again – by my attraction to another woman.

The Sylkie – *for Nicky*

I did not expect her – or what I might feel –
when, like a sylkie, she lifted herself
out of the ocean of London and
onto the rocks of my life.

Unlike anyone before or since,
not of this world and yet totally natural,
soft and frighteningly strong –
I did not know how to be with this creature.

It was the brown eyes that gave her away.
I should have known she would leave me
stranded on the shore
with no way to follow.

This friendship did not last long, as she was Australian and returned home, but it was stimulating enough to help shake me out of my depression. Although I didn't feel sufficiently comfortable with the ambivalence it aroused to pursue another relationship with a woman, certainly some of the assumptions about sexuality I had been indoctrinated with now came into question. I became curious about what was preventing me from finding and expressing my desire for intimate connection. This led me into the, then thriving, world of Encounter Group Therapy. Here I was emotionally opened up wider than I could have imagined, confronted with having to intensely interact with others as well as myself, and met my soon-to-be husband. I understand now it was a bit of a sledgehammer approach and probably not the best environment within which to make life-changing decisions – like who to marry. But that is what I did.

And then Nature decided enough was enough – it was time to have a baby. This was an utterly new and powerful desire. My body opened like a blossom and proved to be fruitful. I now understand how fortunate I was.

Fruition

I am the blossoming apple tree at the bottom of the sea.
My petals float to the surface,
pink flotsam on the shifting surface of Mother Sea.
Deep currents move my branches.
My roots reach into the planet's core.
In the fullness of time a great expedition will set out
in golden bowed boats from the shores of Elysium.
Deep-chested divers will leave the safety of their decks
to plunge down into the sea;
the sweet scent of my ripening fruit drawing them deeper
    and deep,
urgent to harvest the rich, red, heavy fruit.
Only one will reach me.
Only one will feel his hands clasp round the firm flesh.
Only one will rise again, holding the prize,
dripping and triumphant above the surface of the sea.
I am the blossoming apple tree.
I only need to wait.

In quick succession I had two beautiful, healthy, whole children, a boy and a girl, who have been the greatest joys in my life. I opened unreservedly to them – and still do.

Wings of Desire – *for Alice*

Standing in weak winter sunshine
on the draughty floorboards
of our small tied cottage,
I closed my eyes and silently
 called from my heart,
"Are you there?"

To my surprise, you answered
with a soft feather touch on my face –
my desire for you touched
by your desire for me –
this body – this life.

For days after,
in solitary moments,
I felt you fluttering around me –
and then a great calm.

It was no surprise
when the sickness began.
Had you been a boy,
your name would have been
Gabriel.

Motherhood took me deeper inside myself than I had ever been, and I have since learned to use that experience to feed my spiritual as well as my emotional life. It also brought me into a powerful and, at that time, unfamiliar awareness of being in a body – a woman's body. The processes of pregnancy, birth and motherhood were overwhelming. They altered my whole chemistry again and left me vulnerable in the world, without a sense of who I was. I remember feeling myself as invisible behind my baby at a mother-and-baby morning. I was certainly not the young woman I had been (a façade hiding a lonely child) – nor was I a mature woman, confident in her embodied self. I found myself descending again into depression and was told that this was post-natal depression – a common experience. Why was it common? What was actually happening to me?

Adrienne Rich speaks powerfully and poignantly about this dilemma of early motherhood in her book *Of Woman Born*, published only a few years before my first child was born. It was seminal reading in my efforts to try to understand what was going on. As soon as I started it, I felt a resonance with my own experience.

I had no idea of what I wanted, what I could or could not choose.[9]

I had been trying to give birth to myself; and in some grim, dim way I was determined to use even pregnancy and parturition in that process.[10]

> *It is not enough to let our children go; we need selves of our own to return to.*[11]

And especially:

> *I remember thinking I would never dream again (the unconscious of the young mother – where does it entrust its messages, when dream-sleep is denied her for years?)*[12]

Rich's book helped me begin to set my experience in an historical, socio-political context, but some of it frightened me – like her chapter on maternal violence – and it didn't seem to help me understand how to deal with my own personal situation. I had become disconnected from my inner life. Since my early twenties, my dreams had been a source of meaning-making, creativity and inner connection. My first boyfriend had introduced me to the theories of Carl Jung and I found the Jungian approach to dreams and the inner life resonated for me in making sense of my own experience – symbolically through images. But then, like Rich, I lost my dreams.

Shortly after reading *Of Woman Born*, I discovered another book, Nor Hall's *The Moon and The Virgin*[13]. It was published the same year that my son was born. I don't even remember now how it was that I found these books. They found me. Nor Hall, a Jungian therapist, introduced me to a way of looking at my depression as a feminine initiatory experience – going into the dark and eventually emerging, profoundly changed. I owe her a deep debt of gratitude. She introduced me to the myth of Eros and Psyche and to the image of a caterpillar going into a death-like chrysalis state in order to transform into a butterfly – both are metaphors for feminine initiation. Gradually, my dreams came back.

As I began to understand more about what was happening to me, I had enough wisdom to seek help, and the luck to find, some wise people. One of them was a movement psychotherapist, Ruth Noble, who introduced me to the transformational potential of simple movement of the body, supported by and released through the breath. This was powerfully connecting for me and has remained in my life ever since – breath, body and being. It released energy – and desire returned.

Rising

Dark clouds have been gathering all afternoon.
My daughter and her friend are playing in the garden,
where sheets and pillowcases hang along the path.
The air is still and sound seems to be in a vacuum –
little girl voices at the bottom by the wall.
I have been domestic the whole day.
There is an energy rising.
When the lightning comes,
my voice triumphantly invites the thunder to follow.
The girls run across the grass to the house, squealing.

Since writing this poem, and long after the experience it depicts, I found another book by Nor Hall about the Mysteries of Dionysus as depicted on a series of frescos preserved in Pompeii. The frieze, all around the walls of a small ritual chamber, shows stages in a feminine initiation experience. What Hall describes further illuminates what was happening that day in the garden when I spontaneously called out loud, "Come thunder! Come lightning!"

> They responded to the earth-shaking din of the god's call by calling him with loud shouts of "Come!"[14]

> Dionysus is the Shaker, the Loosener. He is that trembling energy that shakes the maenad loose from the confines of complacence...it is marriage that trembles when Dionysus approaches.[15]

> So it begins in the life of a woman who is wanting. She does not want for a man, nor for a child. She wants to be filled like a cornucopia past the point of overflow. The issue is emptiness of the sort that grows from the inside out regardless of one's productivity, like hunger when it is for love or creative work or some other soul food.[16]

My desire to be a woman, embodied and aware, then took me on a journey that has included dramatherapy, Gestalt therapy, psychodrama, Buddhist meditation and Joged Amerta movement. But as I began to change, emerge from the chrysalis, my marriage to my children's father collapsed. I knew I was wanting more and I wrote him a note saying I wanted a passionate affair with my husband. But he was changing too – and his attention went elsewhere. A friend I confided in warned me that someone was bound to notice I was lonely and would want to move in closer to me – and she was right. My woman's body was awake and wanting more of the joy in my life that Lourde describes. My dreams warned me, and Nor Hall describes the maenad as "licked by fire"[17]. Although I wrote the poem below years later, after my ex-husband's death, the dream in it comes from the time just before I realised what was happening.

Fire

I dreamed of smoke rising
between the floor boards
by our bed.
I dreamed I could not wake you.
You once told a friend
I was a fire
you could warm yourself on –
and I was.

But you left the fire untended
and it burned our home down.

Now, cooled by age and loss, tenderly,
my fingers run through the ashes.

I did, indeed, meet someone who wanted to come closer and my desire suddenly had a channel for expression. There was such joy and aliveness in me when Eros burst through into my life, once Dionysus had done his job. This did not feel like my earlier experiences of intimate desire. For all its difficulties and complications, I felt deeply embodied in this relationship. Although it had taken me forty years, there was no going back. Finally, sexual desire found its place in my being – my body not separate from my heart and my inner daemon.

Abundance

Woman's love has come upon me, tiger-like,
full and fierce –
ripening like the grain –
flowing rich and warm like wine,
like blood, like the sea –
all around me, near me, in me,
through me.
Abundance is mine.
I can dance with open arms,
open body, open legs –
taking in and giving out woman's love –
gentle, tender, soft,
holding me and leaving me free.

This poem, while expressing the excitement of that time, is overly optimistic. I was not really free. The impact of my childhood isolation still exerted its influence and needed to be slowly brought to light, understood and healed. But it was a remarkable new beginning. The ending of my first marriage was cataclysmic and, as with all the great changes in my life, required me to undergo the rite of depression. This time, I understood more what was happening and why. I not only suffered it, but consciously learned from it. And I knew more what I wanted in my life and that it was possible for me to have it.

Returning

I have wanted to lie down in a muddy field –
to have rain dissolve my bones and my flesh –
to become earth again.

I have wanted my body to be carried by a river
out onto the sea – shifted like driftwood –
above the deep wet.

I have wanted to stretch and thin out –
the wind to blow through me – my cell walls to open
like wings to the air.

Fleeing like Daphne, this longing to shape-shift –
turn away from the fire – has never endured.
I return to desire.

So where have I got to in terms of my desire in the context of being a woman? Certainly that erotic connection that allows "the open and fearless underlining of my capacity for joy" that Audre Lourde describes is now available to me – if I open to it. I feel it in my connection to the natural world, in my relationships with other people, in my sensual experience of my own body, and in creative acts of expression, my own and others, like poetry, dance, music and theatre. There is real joy and desire in my wanting to deepen to being alive. The simple can be profound. But there is so much more needed to be done for desire and joy to become the birthright experience of women around the world.

Returning to the question that seems to so puzzle men – What do women want? I can only answer this for myself, but I think other women will see something of themselves in what I say, as I draw on my reading and my friends as well as personal experience. Men, also, may see some of their own desires here. I am aware that sexual desire in my life, with the brief exception of my friendship with Nicky, has been within the male/female experience. But my assertion about women and men below will, I hope, resonate with those whose gender identity lies outside this binary.

- We want our own voice and to be listened to – have an equal place at the table – in lovemaking, in discussions, in creating and decision-making.
- We want our unique sensibilities, abilities, experience and understanding available to be drawn from – and the female gaze to be part of any evaluation or exploration.
- We want our passion, our strength of feeling, to be accepted and honoured – so we can be as big as we feel we need to be, without being told we are 'too much', 'aggressive' or 'overly emotional'.
- We want full access to the world of experience, both natural and cultural, so we can enjoy, learn, create and express ourselves.
- We want to be as healthy as possible, mentally and physically – and to make our own choices about what happens to our body.
- We want to be respected, not feared – to be cared about, not patronised.

- We want to feel joy in deep, embodied intimacy – to be desired – and have our desire desired. And we want our willing consent to any intimacy be required and requested – not assumed or tricked into.

- We want to be vulnerable, without being harmed or disempowered. In order to be intimate, we need to be safe enough to open ourselves to another. In fact, we want to be safe enough to access our whole environment, enjoy it and learn from it.

- We want to be allowed to care – not expected to – and have our caring acknowledged.

- Sometimes, we may deeply want to have a baby. Nature is at play here, and if this desire arises it can very strong. A woman is not weaker because of it, but she may be more vulnerable. We want the depth and strength of this desire acknowledged, even though it cannot always be satisfied. Even when it is satisfied, other desires are still there in the picture. It is not everything we want, even though it can seem to be at the time.

Women do not want to be feared, to be dominated or to be side-lined. For this to be possible, men need to take responsibility for their own vulnerability, their own desires, their own inner strength, their own insecurity, their own tenderness, their own fears and neediness and their own potential to adapt, respond and grow.

IMPERMANENCE, DESIRE AND THE NATURAL WORLD

Let me go back to my desire for roses. As I reach for and open to a rose – its beauty and its fragrance – I know it will be a transient experience. The Japanese celebrate this transience in their love of the cherry blossom – sakura – which actually refers to the blossom of all trees in the prunus family. The Japanese aesthetic is deeply informed by impermanence. That, and their animist Shinto religion, drew me to travel to Japan in April 2000 to witness the sakura phenomenon and visit the Shinto shrines of the Kansai peninsula. Shinto shrines, unlike Buddhist temples, are regularly rebuilt from scratch – given new life. I discovered that on the site of every Shinto shrine I visited there was a small Buddhist temple, and on the site of every Buddhist temple, there was a small Shinto shrine. I was told that the Japanese refer themselves to Shintoism for all matters to do with life, and to Buddhism for the matters of death. There is something about this way of integrating life and death, while also maintaining the difference, that strikes me as elegant – as elegant as Haiku poetry.

> *Dying cricket –*
> *how full of*
> *life, his song.*[1]

I don't want to over-simplify or romanticise Japanese culture. I found many confusing anomalies while there, and they are as guilty of damaging the natural environment as anyone else, but the simultaneous desire for life and understanding of impermanence and death I found in Japanese religion, art and poetry has made a deep impression on me.

I remember clearly the thought that prompted my retirement from my teaching job in a special school – "I want to feel fully alive before I am dead!" The work that had been so stimulating was now draining me of energy for doing anything else. This thought took me back to when I first read Marion Milner's book, *A Life of One's Own*, twenty years earlier. I was sitting on a train and, looking up from my book at the landscape through the window, I suddenly felt overcome with longing, knowing I was not quite able to connect with being fully alive in the way she described. I realised that, now almost sixty, I still had not been able to deeply and reliably feel this connection in the way I wanted – this spurred me on to give in my resignation.

So when do I feel most alive? The answer to this is immediate – it's when I am outdoors, taking the time to consciously open myself to the experience of the natural world that is available there – like seeing dolphins in the wild, or skinny dipping in the sea off Kefalonia, or walking out on Dartmoor, or my first visitation by goldcrests.

Birthday Walk

Today is my birthday.
I have been breathing air
for sixty-seven years,
but today my lungs feel new.
My legs are strong
as I climb the hill where
silvered clouds silhouette
a dark lacework of trees.
On my right the moor
holds the whole horizon.

As I cross the farm track
a magpie's sudden chatter
reminds me there is also
grief, pain, violence and fear –
but not here, not now.
Here the grass is shining.
Here love rides the wind
and the sharp air is
full of blessings.

And then –
I see the goldcrest –
inches from me –
a tiny, feathered jewel –
then another – and a third,
casually dropping from twig to twig
while my heart threatens
to break with their beauty.

There are also times of intense and fulfilling connection with another person but, for most of my life, the natural world has been my refuge and life enhancing resource. My desire has focused on the reliable sense of connection I find there – and it is nature that most inspires my poetry. Andreas Weber speaks of "the connection between the transformative power that is part of our living experience and the imaginative power of poetry"[2].

> *Because we are alive, we can comprehend the living universe. We comprehend it by entering into relationship with it – which is to say, by transforming it and allowing it to transform us. And for us, language serves as an instrument of that transformation.*[3]

Mary Oliver reminds us, "Poetry is one of the ancient arts, and it began, as did all the fine arts, within the original wilderness of the earth".[4]

Desire is so much about life – but, as Rob Burbea maintains, it is not just the experience of the life force. Eros is "a wanting of more contact with, penetration of, connection, intimacy, opening to a beloved object"[5] – like a rose. Life, and the eros of life, rises and falls with the seasons. We are part of this cyclical connection of life, loss, death and rebirth – Spring, Summer, Autumn and Winter can all be experienced through the lens of eros. The natural world becomes the other – our object of beauty and desire. The sense of constant change and reliable return can soften our awareness of impermanence and death.

Breakfast in the Garden

In the shade of the flowering cherry
the bird seed is greedily greeted.
I sit warming my winter-chilled back,
my silhouette framing
the soft boiled egg on the table in front of me,
when the shadows around shift –
start to dance to some undetected tune.

Do the birds hear it?
Is the sun dancing –
casting shadows back
and forth across the grass?
Or is the garden, itself, stepping out –
renouncing its long fast –
announcing an appetite for April?

June

At this time of year
there are some evenings
when everything seems
to glow from within.
The sun takes a back seat
and the world itself shines.

The birch tree glows,
shivering light from every leaf.
Grass floats in a pool of luminosity.
Pansies shine up from their pot,
and the muted nicotiana
becomes vibrant.

My skin seems translucent
and anyone watching me
sitting on this bench
should be able to see
the pulsing radiance
of my heart.

Autumn Sunrise

As honeyed light daubs
the hedgerow trees
one at a time
seemingly at random,
damp webs of mist
long lying unseen in darkness
begin to shift and rise.

The wide yellowing hands
of the great plane tree
are lit up slowly –
a few at a time –
and the oak's black limbs
become outlined in
luminescence.

The rooks have been awake
for a while, sallying
purposefully back and forth.
Now they have gathered again
for an audience with each other,
their grinding harmonies
rising and falling.

The distant hillfort
stays dark – shadowed –
while the fields below
are leisurely laid out in light.

Maybe the ancient ones,
resting up there
under a thick duvet
of sycamore and elm,
are having a lie-in
this morning.

November's Trees

I have been watching the trees
loosening their hold on the leaves.
At first I saw only the leaves –
their myriad movements, shapes
and mutable colours.
The wind arrived, pushing and pulling.
Some leaves were torn off.
Others gave up and let go.

Rain and wind came and went.
Rain came and went.
More leaves dropped away.
Over the days, the branches emerged,
dark and wet, each shaped by
particulars of place, species,
time and weather.

This morning the woods are quiet.
So many empty branches!
The energy of the upright trees
has moved inwards towards
heartwood and deep roots.
There is only a breath of breeze.
The air around each twig
is cold, sharp and clear.

As a child, the natural world was a place to escape to – to leave behind the confusing and unsafe world of human beings. Birds, particularly have always caught my imagination – because of the sense of freedom that the power of flight inspires. Birds can seem both earthly and heavenly others – divine, even.

Bird Life

If I could,
I would go to sleep and wake when the birds do.
Sometimes I would gather garrulously with my kind
like sparrows or starlings –
but, as with albatross,
mate just once – for life.
I would hover over the spaces of my mind,
patiently alert and curious
as a kestrel over a field.
Just as demoiselle cranes cross the Himalayas,
I would risk and rise over the greatest obstacles –
echo my sadness over the surface of the night
like a loon over the lake –
and I would tread lightly on the earth like a wren –
leaving no more trace when I die
than a few feathers and fine bones.

A Secret
Psst…lean closer.
I have been given a secret
and the duty to share it.
But take care.
If you do not want
your ground to be shaken,
your heart to be broken and
your soul to open,
close your eyes now
and cover your ears.

All birds are angels.
Every time you see, hear or sense them,
it is a Visitation and Annunciation.

Now that you know,
what gaps might appear in your life?
and what might fly through?

When doing research into fear, I learned that curiosity plays an important role in our ability to regulate our fear. The natural world, and my desire for it, has offered me a stage on which to enact my endless imaginative curiosity, and thereby strengthen my resilience.

Stalking – *for Nigel*

I am stalking beauty
in a midsummer garden –
on the alert for what is hidden
or possibly just overlooked,
like dark specks on a thistle flower,
revealed as nose-down
bottle-green beetles, gorging.

Silence and stillness bring rewards.

A window opens up

into a blackthorn bush where
two warbler fledglings are leaning
their soft bodies against each other.
One stretches a wing,
its tiny insectivorous beak
rummaging in fluffy feathers.

Hedgehog Journey

There's a hedgehog in our garden.
I leave offerings of cat biscuits
and fresh water.
I built it a house, covered in leaves
I found scattered about like
yellow and bronze dinosaur footprints.
And then I leave it alone.
They are solitary, night-creeping creatures,
not fond of company.

Really – I want to follow it as
it stretches its pencil-point nose
out into the moist loamy darkness.
I want to trundle behind it
across the muddied grass,
avoiding pools of light from the house,
and head for where snails collect
under cracked rims of old flower pots
on the gravel yard.

I have spotted it here. But
I want to go where it goes after.
I want to push through the hedgehog-sized
gap under the fence.
I want to feel the wood brush over my bristles,
the earth slip under my soft belly.
I want to run on
my four dainty feet
across the neighbour's lawn.

My Buddhist meditation practice has greatly enhanced my desire for and engagement with nature.

Presence – *after Denise Levertov*

I listen to my breath
as if it were not mine –
the inhalation and exhalation
of a sea all around me.

I can let my bones
go for a walk –
wrapped in muscle and skin –
flesh in motion.

I open my eyes
to veins on leaves
and stretch marks on bark
as if I was not there –
only a tree being tree.

And I am learning to
reach out my hands to another –
not to touch – or be touched –
but to love.

Not insouciant like an armadillo –
but present – sensing presence.

Distraction

When walking in the woods
I want to be
intensely distracted –
each sound,
each movement,
each form pushing itself
into being around me.
Progress will be slow.
I am not going anywhere.

My desire to connect with the natural world has given me, right from the beginning, an experiential understanding of change, loss, death and decay. These are everywhere in life. Sometimes I have looked at it all with the wondrous, compassionate enthusiasm of Walt Whitman – as if death is only more life.

> *What do you think has become of the young and the old men?*
> *What do you think has become of the women and children?*
> *They are alive and well somewhere:*
> *The smallest sprout shows there is really no death,*
> *And if ever there was it led forward to life and does not wait at the*
> *end to arrest it,*
> *And ceased the moment life appeared.*[6]

But does this really reflect my experience of death and its effect on desire? Impermanence and death can bring up a great deal of sadness and longing.

His Jacket

In your bedroom, hanging up on the picture rail, is your jacket.
Taking it down, I recognise the old wooden hanger
still with the shop label – Mr Fish.
You once worked there – in London – long before we met.
Has this jacket ever been cleaned?
It's been worn – more than once:
good woollen cloth – no matching trousers –
imprinted with the shape of your shoulders and elbows –
some remnants of a meal gently staining the lapels.
If I press it to my face, will I still recognise the smell of your
  skin –
twenty-eight years after we parted?
Our daughter is watching. She would understand, but she
  might cry.
She tells me it goes into the charity shop bag.

You always knew

You always knew it was going to be like this –
the years rolling in like waves
immersing you,
then pulling back to reveal more and more
as the tide gradually recedes –
leaving you beached,
picking up bits and pieces left behind,
rolling them round in your hands
as you try to remember –
try to understand.
Now the tide is coming back in
faster than you would like.
And you know that when the waves recede again
you will no longer be here.

But, the awareness of death can also bring up a fierce desire for life – now, while I am alive – and a determination to express my desire without the cultural curbs I used to experience.

Hag

Hag-ag-ag-ag-ag-ag-ag…
I am beautiful – do you see?
I don't give a fuck if you don't,
but don't go thinking you can see like me.
I am looking through my skin, my bones, my belly and my
     heart.
Yes – there is more and more loss.
But I am still here. And then, I will be gone –
your loss, not mine.
I will take my losses with me –
and leave my beauty behind
for you to find.

My Mouth is an Organ of Desire

I love lipstick.
The colour must match
my earrings.

I pull the top off with a click –
rotating to reveal
a moistly soft pillar of pink
rising to greet me.

I slide it over parted lips –
pressing those lips together,
neatly and generously –
pouting and smiling in the mirror
to check the effect.

It's a ritual invitation
to consume and be consumed –
an invocation of consummation.

And then there is the reality of death. It is has come for many I love and it will come for me.

> *The message of a world in which all things interpenetrate and consume one another in order to affirm and to realize their desire of more being is not one of universal nonviolence. On the contrary: This world is a tragic universe precisely because it is creation in the genuine sense, because the act of creation is being consummated in every moment, because this world is inwardly alive and is therefore constantly producing real deaths every second, one of which will assuredly be ours someday.[7]*

My deep desire to be fully alive will not prevail against this – nor would I want it to. To be fully alive means to embrace death and its 'tragedy'.

Expugno – *for Julia*

"Expugno!" she whispers,
mustering her fragile breath.
Uncertain, I lean further forward.
"I have been taken by storm!"
The ramparts are breached.
Death is within the walls.

Queen of the Tips,
she knew how to seek and find,
mend, gild, polish and place,
filling each room in her castle
with refashioned relics
garlanded in green.

Artist and Dreamer,
in solitary sensuality,
she would suspend herself
over a bluebell sea,
or breathe the air
of midnight moonlight.

Her attendants lay her
under a rose petal shroud
on high, grassy ramparts,
flanked by towers of
lime, ash and beech.
Above her the swift flies.

May Life take me by storm
before Death does.
Open the gates!
Let the walls fall!
Sun in the courtyard!
Wind in the hall!

While writing this book, Prapto died. He has been so important to my exploration of body, movement and desire. Embracing death takes me into my familiar response to deep change – inwards to wait, without desire, until I emerge again – or not.

When Desire is Not Enough

When desire is not enough –
when the train has left the station,
the expectant traveller stranded alone
on an empty platform and
the heart says, *there is nothing*
here for me now –
when there is no possibility of returning,
the desired destination unattainable –
then an unexpected stillness arrives
and opens its doors –
destination uncertain.

Choose to step on board
carrying your open, aching heart.

OPENING THE GATES – Part One

Very early on in my enquiry into deep desire I found myself drawn to the story of 'The Descent of Inanna to the Great Below', a Sumerian myth written down in cuneiform script on clay tablets about 4,000 years ago. Sumer, as a distinct land and culture, was already 1,000 years old by then, having emerged over millennia in an area where agriculture first began – what is now southern Iraq. It was able to develop there because these people discovered how to irrigate the land. Although Sumer had two great rivers running through it, the Tigris and the Euphrates, it was basically desert-like. For drinking water, people relied on deep wells. Once they understood how to irrigate their fields, increasing the yield of their crops, cities were eventually able to develop and, with them, an elaborate and highly sophisticated culture, including art, music and literature. It is this culture that is so beautifully evidenced in the clay tablets. For my understanding of this story I drew on two translations: S N Kramer's[1] and the University of Oxford's 'Electronic Text Corpus of Sumerian Literature'[2].

The first stirrings happened when I was asked in a poetry class to try to write from the point of view of a mythological character. Ereshkigal popped immediately into my mind, despite my not having thought of this myth for many years. The poem came out as a whole in a ten-minute writing exercise and has not needed to be changed or developed since. This rarely happens for me. As I reflected on Ereshkigal's words, I wondered, "What desire led Inanna into attempting to do such a deadly dangerous thing as to enter the underworld of the dead, where her powerful sister, Ereshkigal, ruled as Queen?" Inanna was the Queen of Heaven and Earth, the Great Above. In cosmology she was the morning and the evening star, shining and beautiful. She was dynamic, passionate and overtly sexual – desire itself. She was also the goddess of war, fierce in the defence of her people. At the time Inanna decided to take this journey, she was no longer a young goddess. She was in the fullness of her power. Her consort was Dumuzi, the great Shepherd-God, King of Uruk, Inanna's special city. She had two grown sons, both of whom were kings in other cities. She had the love of her people and many temples devoted to her.

The Descent is clearly a myth of the cycles of nature, of the connection between birth and death, reflected in the processes of sowing, growing and harvesting grain. But, like all great stories, it comes across as more complex than that, with many possible layers of meaning. It is a shamanic journey, where wisdom is brought back from the underworld at great cost. It has been given the Jungian treatment as a story of psychological transformation.[3] I, myself, have used it to help a therapy client make sense of her depression. On another level the story can be seen as a family drama. Sumerian mythology has a family structure and the characters are all enmeshed in close relationships. Ereshkigal is Inanna's sister. Enki, who as the God of Wisdom and of the Deep, Sweet Waters is a key element in the outcome of the story, is their maternal grandfather. Nanna is Inanna's father and Enlil is her paternal grandfather. Inanna's close servant, advisor, companion and friend is Ninshubur, a Queen from the East in her own right. My interest was to look at the story from the perspective of desire. What did Inanna feel she wanted? It must have been a deep desire for her to take such a huge risk. Did she know what she wanted? – or was there just a deep 'wanting'?

At the beginning of the story, Inanna "opened her ear to the Great Below. She set her mind on the Great Below". Samuel Noah Kramer, who was one of the translators of the tablets, tells us that the word for 'ear' is the same as the word for 'wisdom' in Sumerian, and that it can also mean 'mind'. And he says that the word translated as 'opened' can mean 'set'. Inanna specifically set (opened) her mind (ear) on the Great Below.[4] What motivated her to do this and what she felt about it are not told, although, given the choice of words, the desire for wisdom or knowing seems to have been part of it. She just determined to go. The story also speaks in terms of abandonment. She abandons her people and her temples. She abandons the Great Above. She leaves everything behind her to make this journey.

She prepares by taking to herself the seven 'me', her divine powers, in the form of the garments she wears. Then she calls for Ninshubur and together they make their way to the Gates of the Underworld. There, Inanna tells Ninshubur she needs her to wait outside the gates for her return. If she doesn't come out in three days, Ninshubur is to take on all the attributes and garments of mourning and go to Inanna's powerful grandfather, Enlil, and ask him to intervene. If he refuses, then she is to go to Nanna, Inanna's father, for help. If this proves fruitless as well, then she must go to Enki, because "He knows the secrets" and will know what to do.

Then Inanna knocks loudly on the gates, which are guarded by the gatekeeper, Neti. He doesn't understand why anyone would voluntarily want to come in and asks her, "Why has your heart led you on the road from which no traveller returns?" Inanna announces it is because of her sister, Ereshkigal – and because she wants to witness the funeral rites of her sister's husband, The Bull of Heaven. This last seems spurious to me and is never mentioned again, although it may indicate that Inanna does not want to die, only to see. The first, however, rings true – she wants to see her sister. But why, and why now? Here may lie the family drama. Whatever the reason, Ereshkigal is not pleased when Neti brings her the news that her sister is outside the gate, demanding entrance. Basically, she is being put into the position of having to commit sororicide. She tells Neti that he is to allow Inanna through the gates, all seven of them, but he must only lift each gate a little, so that she must crouch down in order to enter – and he is to remove one of her garments each time, thus divesting her of her divine powers. The first time this happens, Inanna is indignant – but Neti firmly tells her that she is not to question the ways of the underworld. It seems to me that it must have been at this point, before which Inanna is every inch the proud and powerful goddess, that she realises the journey will not be on her own terms. By the time she reaches Ereshkigal, Inanna is naked and on her knees.

Inanna

Unlike the burning passion
I know so well –
hot, sticky and raging –
this desire rose cool and sharp
from deep inside me –
to see her, to touch her and know.
It would not let me rest.

I knew it would be risky
to go to my sister's house,
so I left explicit instructions
with the woman I trusted most.
Even if the others refused,
the old man by the water
would not let me down.

Pierced through by longing
to hear her dark secrets,

the deeper I went
the less of me there was.
And when I looked up
into her obsidian eyes.
I knew I would know.

Ereshkigal

She wanted to come –
my beautiful, sparkling sister –
to visit me.
From where she danced in the sky –
kissing the moon –
she could not see me,
so failed to understand.
As much as I loved her, she needed to know
she could not just drop in for a chat.

So I stripped her of all her pretty things.
She could have turned back,
but she always was game for a lark –
up for a dare. Even as a child
she would lead the way –
lifting up latches of doors
we were not meant to enter –
peering into places
we were not meant to see.

Here, I am in charge and I know this place.
The mysteries of darkness and death
are in my care –
not for the curious.
When finally she arrived –
naked and expectant –
I pulled off her shining skin
and hung up her dripping body.
She needed to understand her limits.

Outside the gates, Ninshubur waits the allotted three days, and then carefully follows the instructions Inanna has given her. Both Enlil and Nanna refuse to intervene, maintaining that Inanna well understands that going to "the Dark City" is a one-way trip. It is interesting that in both translations these gods describe Inanna as having "craved" the Great Below – they believed she desired something there. Ninshubur has to place all her hopes onto Enki.

Ninshubur

I did not want her to go.
But when she told me to stand guard –
to hold vigil – I thought:
I am a woman.
I know how to wait.

Her father and grandfather
dared not come between
these two puissant sisters.
I saw fear in their eyes,
and felt rage and despair.

So to the deep, sweet water
I walked and sat down.
I tore at my hair, called out my grievance.
The old man received me with
kindness and tears – then set to work.

Enki

I heard her pain and grief
long before word arrived –
my skin tightened –
my bones ached.
This dark, solemn sister,
so aware of necessity,
knew she had no choice.

I remember them both
in my heart's mind.
My fingers remember
the touch of their hair –
one like a raven's wing –
the other, liquid light.
Two hearts beating in time.

Long separated –
co-existence not an option –
it was only a matter of time
before the shining one,
so full of possibility,
would seek the other out.
I choose to heal them both.

Enki pulls a little bit of dirt from under a fingernail on one of his hands and fashions it into a tiny being, with no gender, and he calls it a Kugara. Then he pulls a little bit of dirt from under a fingernail on his other hand and fashions it into another tiny being, with no gender, and he calls it a Galatura. To the Kugara he gives the Water of Life and to the Galatura he gives the Food of Life. He tells them to swiftly go down to the Gates of the Underworld and squeeze under them. He says they will not be noticed because they are too small and they have no gender. When they come into the presence of Ereshkigal, they will find her in great pain and unattended. When she cries out, they must cry out too. When she groans, they are to groan with her. When she moans, they must moan too. Then she will notice them, and she will be grateful that her pain has been witnessed and shared. She will offer them a reward – anything they desire from all the riches of the world. But they are to refuse everything she offers, and ask only for the body up on the hook – and she will give it to them.

Kugara and Galatura

We are Enki's emissaries.
We are not much – a pinch of dirt each.
Like flies we flit to and through the dark gates.
We are not much – a pinch of dirt each.

It's life we carry – and the old man's love.
We are not much – a pinch of dirt each.
She's alone and unaided - we come to her side.
We are not much – a pinch of dirt each.

We hear her cry out – we hear her groan.
We are not much – a pinch of dirt each.
We hear her pain – take her pain as our own.
We are not much – a pinch of dirt each.

She is birthing in death and dying in birth.
We are not much – a pinch of dirt each.
We echo her cries and offer our tears.
We are not much – a pinch of dirt each.

She's no longer alone – no longer unheard.
We are not much – a pinch of dirt each.
She blesses our presence, gives us the dead.
We are not much – a pinch of dirt each.

Both queens are restored by the water of life.
We are not much – a pinch of dirt each.
Revived to themselves, healed of their strife.
We are not much – a pinch of dirt each.

The smallest of gestures can cross deep divides.
It need not be much – a glance or a word.
I'm here and I see you – I'm touched by your pain.
Empathy's emissaries.

And so Inanna is restored to life by the intercession of Enki's tiny beings, and she begins her journey back to the Great Above. I want to leave the story there. What comes next is rich and interesting, but it doesn't shed any more light on what desire drew Inanna to make the descent in the first place. I told this story, including reciting the poems, to an audience at Wootton Fitzpaine Village Hall in Dorset. It was well received and, afterwards, I asked them what deep desire they thought led Inanna to go on such a dangerous journey. Some answers were along the family drama line, the sister-thing, some along the more shamanic line and many along the line of the need to bring together the opposites of light and dark, life and death. A child in the audience said she thought Inanna had become dissatisfied with having everything she wanted, and desired to know what it was like to have nothing.

Of course, all of these answers are valid but I think, in a sense, the child is right. Inanna was filled to the brim with the delights of heaven and earth. It was what she knew and she felt confident and powerful there. But she did not know death. She was aware of death, but had no deep knowledge of it. She must have sensed the power of it – something she could not get at – could not understand. This left her with a compelling, insistent curiosity and desire. The desire for the underworld is about what you want and don't know, not about what you know and want. It involves that intense sense of wanting to penetrate something you feel is there somewhere, just out of sight, just out of reach. It requires going deeply inwards, into the dark. It requires you to give up self and the power that self has relied on. The stripping of Inanna's divine powers from her is required.

There are times in life when death reaches out and touches you. Then the need, the desire even, wells up inside to understand what it really means. From childhood onwards, it has come up many times in my life – death's existential mystery. Sometimes it has been just a soft brushing past and sometimes it has been a hard blow. Since the death of my parents and then of several friends, mostly younger than me, combined with the undeniable aging of my own body, my awareness of the nearness and elusiveness of death appears on an almost daily basis.

I am beginning to see that my investigations into fear, creativity, vulnerability and desire over the last seven years have all been, to some extent, a response to this call from the Great Below. But I have also been passionately listening to the call of the Great Above. I hear it in the song and flight of birds, see it in the soft look in another's eyes, feel it in the shock of moorland or sea air in my lungs. Deep desire is about life and, for me, about wanting to feel fully alive. I don't think Inanna wanted to lose her life. It's more like she wanted to add death to her life. I think my conscious exploration of my own fear, vulnerability and desire have further enabled me to open the gates – and these gates have levels of meaning, just like the story of Inanna has. My deep desires are around feeling fully connected to my place in being. This includes both death and life.

OPENING THE GATES – Part Two

My own journey through gates has been different from that of Inanna, although I can identify with hers at times. In the posts on my blog[1] about many different kinds of desire, I am noticing a theme in my process. The word that expresses this theme is CONNECTION. Inanna was intimately in touch with life, but desired to connect with her sister – the unknown shadow to life, which is death. Growing through desire has been about daring to open my gates to life, others and the world. Sometimes, there have been times of being thrust back behind them. Sometimes, an opening has been sudden and overwhelming, leading to a withdrawal, but I celebrate that I have persevered.

I think my longing, and ultimately desire, for connection arose at my birth, due to an experience of separation that was impossible to understand and integrate at the time. Perhaps the general human existential longing for connection begins with the birth experience. I don't know, but I think mine did. Thinking deeply enough about this as a young woman made me passionate about not being separated from my babies when they were both born. But there is another theme emerging alongside which relates to the desire for connection and ties into my earlier enquiries into fear – the desire to open the gates. By this I mean the gates inside that defend me from the perceived threats of existence – defend my vulnerability. There can be no intimacy, no deep connection, without vulnerability. If any of the inner gates are closed, connection has been limited. What I see in my own writing is this DEEP DESIRE TO OPEN, so that I can touch and be touched, as I express in in my poem 'Longing is Not Desire'.

My gates have protected me when I felt intolerably vulnerable – but they became habits. Habitual defences are difficult to detect, easier to see in another than in yourself. If you don't know they are there, the gates will stay closed. Finding my way through my gates has been happening since I first became aware of the longing to connect as a small child. A sad feeling of separateness is maybe the first clue I had of being closed off – what I am now seeing as being behind gates. It was all a very instinctive, unconscious journey until, due to recurrent depression, I began looking at this feeling more directly in Encounter Groups during my late twenties. Through the years I have explored many different approaches to opening my gates, so many I don't want to list them all here. It has required me to look at what is unknown and frightening – to risk being vulnerable. In Inanna's story, she finally understood complete, ultimate vulnerability – death.

Well after I had written the poems for the Descent of Inanna, two and a half years after the writing of 'Ereshkigal', I had an experience where my gates were flung wide open and I was rendered almost helpless. 'Longing is Not Desire' was written almost exactly a year before this happened. One might wonder what I had invited into my life. I had a fall which resulted in a deep wound in the back of my leg, followed by a mini-stroke. It left me with almost no energy, no words, and no thoughts for weeks. This was a descent in the sense that my body was thrown into trauma, and I was stripped of my usual powers. I just lay still. I was aware that my mind seemed empty and my body barely moved, except when it shook uncontrollably. This happened at intervals for several days and nights. I knew this was the shock gradually discharging and just watched it happening. I felt more vulnerable than I have ever remembered feeling, but I felt no fear at any time. In its place was a free-floating, gentle curiosity. Every other emotion flooded through the open gates – especially love. I had no energy to defend myself against love, and there was a lot of it about. It is only afterwards that I was able to reflect that this traumatic experience was a great healing. My gates had closed when I was very tiny and very vulnerable, and I needed to go back there to repair. There was pain still, but where there had been isolation, I was surrounded by love and care. Where I had felt confusion and fear, I now had enough embodied understanding to trust. I was open and it was good.

During the time of my enquiry into desire, I have been influenced by the Buddhist teacher Rob Burbea. I was attracted by his way of looking at desire as a positive, transformative force.[2] At the start of the Preface to his book on Emptiness, Rob maintains, "Curiosity and desire can be the most precious forces".[3] This strongly resonates with me. I have attended retreats with him and listened to many of his on-line talks, and he keeps asking, "What is it you most deeply want? What's the most important thing?" He also maintains that if you take the time to deeply reflect on this, once you get through the surface desires of the body and the habitual craving of the mind, you will discover that what you most deeply desire is already available. You just have to open to it. This may sound simple, but it has been a long, challenging and, at times, devastating journey for me.

Now in my seventies, after all this time, my gates need to keep being opened. Habit is stubborn, but just to say the word 'open' to myself helps. The instinct of the soul is to open – to be revealed, to make more and more contact. Rob maintains that this is endlessly rich in its potential. The survival instinct can cause us to curl up and hide or run away from contact. That's a very simplistic way of putting it – but it makes sense to me now. There is the need to take care of myself – to take care of my vulnerability. Threats can be real, I know. But sometimes it is necessary to be vulnerable in the face of real threats – as Inanna was – as climate activists are. There is no way to defend against the ultimate threat, anyway. Our choices about this depend on what is really, deeply important to us. That was why I asked what it was Inanna wanted – even though there is no one answer. That is why I keep asking myself what it is I really want. What do I deeply desire?

I want to open more and more. I want to open my body – soften and blur my boundaries, without losing touch with that clear, empty axis within, grounded in earth and reaching up to sky. I want to open my joints and the cells of my body. I want to open all my senses, open my heart, and open my mind.

I want to touch and be touched by everything, however vulnerable that makes me feel – however challenging and difficult. I want to feel connected to it all without losing my sense of being embodied.

Though this connection, I want to feel the uniqueness and beauty of each time, place, being and thing, big and small, gentle and terrible, in and around me, including my own beauty and uniqueness. I want to open to the complexity of all of this without falling into overwhelm.

I want to be filled with love for it all. And I want to express and create from this place – to share it and help others become aware of the precious potential of connection.

This is not too much to ask.

Pure

Light ignites the blackbird,
the first pure note
sung with its whole being.
Loss is my path now.
Perhaps it always was.
Can I open to it every day
as the bird does to light?
Fierce lessons of loss –
bursts of fragile beauty –
nothing remains
in the end
but love.

Afterword

Shortly after completing the draft of this book, and less than five months after Prapto's death, the Buddhist teacher Rob Burbea died. It is my hope that this book honours him. I found him to be truly open in the way I desire to be, in his life and in his death. Although I had known him as the resident teacher at Gaia House for many years, it was not until 2016 that I discovered his teachings on desire. They opened up and super-charged my enquiry. I am still learning from them, and from the rest of the extraordinary body of teachings and teachers he left with us. As he once said, when talking about death and loss, "There is not just loss – there is a gift there". That gift keeps on giving.

REFERENCES

INTRODUCTION

1 https://www.moveintolife.com/

2 http://ecartepublications.co.uk/cultural-landscapes/#p=152

3 Booker, Mary (2015) *Nothing Special: Experiencing fear and vulnerability in daily life*, Triarchy Press

4 Bromberg, Philip M (2011) *Awakening the Dreamer: Clinical journeys*; Routledge, p.119

5 Bakewell, Sarah (2011) *How To Live: A life of Montaigne in one question and twenty attempts at an answer*, Vintage Books

6 Spinelli, Ernesto (1989) *The Interpreted World: An introduction to phenomenological psychology*, Sage Publications

7 https://goingdeeper.uk/

8 Bateson, Nora (2016) *Small Arcs of Larger Circles: Framing through other patterns*, Triarchy Press, p.169

9 Interview with Nora Bateson (12 November 2018) 'Awakening Interdependence and Evolving Systems with Warm Data', EMERGE podcast with Daniel Thorsen, https://bit.ly/Flame21

LOOKING FOR DESIRE
Needs and Desire

1 https://en.wikipedia.org/wiki/Erotes

2 Booker, Mary (2015) *Nothing Special: Experiencing fear and vulnerability in daily life*, Triarchy Press

3 Oliver, Mary (1992) *New and Selected Poems: Vol. One*, Beacon Press; p.65

4 Wohlleben, Peter (2017) *The Hidden Life of Trees, What They Feel, How They Communicate: Discoveries from a secret world*, William Collins

5 'The Tall Guy' (1989) dirs. Richard Curtis and Mel Smith, (film trailer) https://bit.ly/Flame33

Moving – Desire as a Verb

1 Carson, Anne (1998) *Eros: The bittersweet*, Dalkey Archive Press, p.17

2 *Roget's Pocket Thesaurus* (1963) Pocket Books

[3] Irvine, William B (2006) *On Desire: Why we want what we want*, Oxford University Press

[4] https://en.oxforddictionaries.com/definition/want

Lack and Longing

[1] Solnit, Rebecca (2005) *A Field Guide to Getting Lost*, Canongate, p.30

[2] Carson, Anne, *op. cit.* p.10

[3] McLinden, Mike and McCall, Stephen (2002) *Learning Through Touch: Supporting children with visual impairments and additional difficulties*, David Fulton

[4] 'Wings of Desire' (1987) dir. Wim Wenders, (trailer) https://bit.ly/Flame22

Buddhism and Desire

[1] Weber, Andreas (2014) *Matter & Desire: An erotic ecology*, Chelsea Green Publishing, p.16

[2] Peacock, John (August 2012) 'The Mindful Way To Equanimity', talk given at Gaia House, Devon, UK

[3] Loy, David (2000) *Lack and Transcendence: The problem of death and life in psychotherapy, existentialism, and Buddhism*, Humanity Books

[4] Preece, Rob (2000) *The Alchemical Buddha: Introducing the psychology of Buddhist Tantra*, Mudra Publications, pp.v-vi

[5] Epstein, Mark (2006) *Open To Desire: The truth about what the Buddha taught*, Gotham Books, p.136

[6] Suryodarmo, Suprapto (June 2015) personal communication

[7] Suryodarmo, Suprapto (June 2011) personal communication

[8] *Ibid.*

[9] Suryodarmo, Suprapto (June 2015), *op. cit.*

[10] Suryodarmo, Suprapto (July 2016) personal communication

[11] Burbea, Rob (2014) *Seeing That Frees: Meditations on emptiness and dependent arising*, Hermes Amāra Publications

[12] Burbea, Rob (28.03.2017) 'Questions & Answers' in *Of Hermits and Lovers: The alchemy of desire*, https://bit.ly/Flame23

[13] Burbea, Rob (2017) 'Opening Up To The Current of Desire', in *Of Hermits and Lovers: The alchemy of desire*: https://bit.ly/Flame24

[14] *Ibid.*

Greco-Roman Views of Desire

[1] Neumann, Erich (1973) *Amor and Psyche: The psychic development of the feminine*, Bollingen Series LIV, Princeton University Press

[2] Jones, Gwyn (1956) *Scandinavian Legends and Folk-tales*, Oxford University Press. This version is long out of print, but you can read the basic story here: https://fairytalez.com/east-sun-west-moon-2/

[3] Murdock, Maureen (1990) *The Heroine's Journey: Woman's quest for wholeness*, Shambhala. Also: https://bit.ly/Flame30

[4] Ovid, trans. Mary M. Innes (1955) *The Metamorphoses of Ovid*, Penguin Classics

[5] Bateson, Nora (2016) *op. cit.* pp.53-61

[6] *Ibid.* p.61

[7] *Ibid.* p.56

[8] Carson, Anne, *op. cit.* p.11

[9] *Ibid.* p.16

[10] *Ibid.* p.39

[11] *Ibid.* p.44

[12] Plato, trans. Christopher Gill (1999) *The Symposium*, Penguin Classics

[13] *Ibid.* p.xxviii

[14] *Ibid.* p.xvii

[15] *Ibid.* p.48, 210d

[16] Epictetus, trans. & ed. Robert Dobbin (2008) *Discourses and Selected Writings*, Penguin Classics

[17] *Ibid.* 'The Discourses' Book IV, 74, p.183

[18] *Ibid.* 'Fragments', p.222

[19] McGilchrist, Iain (2009) *The Master and his Emissary: The divided brain and the making of the Western world*, Yale University Press, p.269

The Desire to Create

[1] Solnit, Rebecca (2013) *The Faraway Nearby*, Granta Publications, p.185

[2] Burbea, Rob (11.08.2015) 'Love and the Demands of the Imaginal, Part 1' (online talk), https://bit.ly/Flame27

[3] Corbin, Henri (1998) *The Voyage and The Messenger: Iran and philosophy*, North Atlantic Books. This image originally from Exodus 23:20

[4] Winnicott, Donald W. (1991) *Playing and Reality*, Routledge, p.14

[5] Levine, Stephen K. (1997) *Poiesis: The Language of psychology and the speech of the soul*, Jessica Kingsley

[6] *Ibid.* pp.40-41

[7] *Ibid.* p.41

[8] Hewitson, Owen (9 May 2010) *What Does Lacan Say About … Desire?* https://bit.ly/Flame26

[9] Burns, Sarah (09.02.2017) Personal conversation

[10] Plato, trans. Christopher Gill (1999) *The Symposium*, Penguin Classics

[11] Levertov, Denise (1973) *The Poet in the World*, New Directions, p.48

[12] *Ibid.* p.54

[13] Sciamma, Céline (12.02.2020) *Céline Sciamma on Letting Desires Dictate Writing*, with Briony Hanson – https://bit.ly/Flame32

GROWING THROUGH DESIRE

Women and Desire

[1] Lourde, Audre (2019) first published 1984, *Sister Outsider*, Penguin Classics, pp.43-49

[2] *Ibid.* p.117

[3] *Ibid.* p.118

[4] Eltahawy, Mona (31.05.2018) *Sister-hood: Interview with Mona Eltahawy, feminist author and public speaker*, https://bit.ly/Flame28

[5] Jones, Gwyn *op. cit.* Read the stories at https://fairytalez.com/prince-lindworm/ and https://fairytalez.com/the-wild-swans/

[6] https://fairytalez.com/the-red-shoes/

[7] Lourde, Audre, *op. cit.* pp.46-47

[8] Bateson, Nora (2016) *op. cit.* p.169

[9] Rich, Adrienne (1977) *Of Woman Born: Motherhood as experience and institution*, Virago, p.25

[10] *Ibid.* p.29

[11] *Ibid.* p.37

[12] *Ibid.* p.32

[13] Hall, Nor (1980) *The Moon and the Virgin: Reflections on the archetypal feminine,* The Woman's Press

[14] Hall, Nor (2019) *Those Women*, Spring Publications, p.21

[15] *Ibid.* p.29

[16] *Ibid.* pp.42-43

[17] *Ibid.* p.34

Impermanence and Desire
[1] Basho (1985) *On Love and Barley: Haiku of Basho*, Penguin Classics, #228, p.74
[2] Weber, Andreas, *op. cit.* p.88
[3] *Ibid.*, p.89
[4] Oliver, Mary (1994) *A Poetry Handbook: A prose guide to understanding and writing poetry*, Harcourt Publishing, p.106
[5] Burbea, Rob (26.03.2017) *The Problem of Desire* in *Of Hermits and Lovers: The alchemy of desire*: https://bit.ly/Flame25
[6] Whitman, Walt (1855) *Song of Myself* [6] from *Leaves of Grass*, Penguin
[7] Weber, Andreas, *op. cit.* p.66

Opening the Gates
Part One
[1] https://bit.ly/3BABheC
[2] https://bit.ly/Flame29
[3] Perera, Sylvia B. (1881) *Descent to the Goddess: A way of initiation for women*, Inner City Books
[4] Wolkstein, Diane & Kramer, Samuel N. (1983) *Inanna, Queen of Heaven and Earth: Her stories and hymns from Sumer*, Harper & Row

Part Two
[1] https://goingdeeper.uk
[2] https://dharmaseed.org/retreats/3270
[3] Burbea, Rob (2014) *op. cit.*

ABOUT THE AUTHOR

Mary Booker was born in Ithaca, New York, of an English father and an American mother. She has been living in England since 1971, where she trained as a teacher and then as a dramatherapist.

Mary has practised dramatherapy with a wide range of client groups for almost thirty years, twenty-five of which she was also lecturer and trainer on the Devon-based MA in Dramatherapy. For eleven years she worked in special education as a multi-sensory impairment specialist, and wrote about this work in her book, *Developmental Drama: Dramatherapy Approaches for People with Profound or Severe Multiple Disabilities, Including Sensory Impairment* (Jessica Kingsley).

Mary lives in Exeter with her husband, Chris. Being retired now, she is free to devote herself to meditation and movement practice, writing, and walking in the woods, at the sea and on the moor. She is a member of Exeter Extinction Rebellion and the XR Devon Drummers.

ABOUT THE PUBLISHER

Triarchy Press is an independent publisher of original and alternative thinking about organisations and government, financial and social systems (and how to make them work better) and human beings and the ways in which they participate in the world – moving, walking, thinking, dreaming, suffering and loving.

www.triarchypress.net

Lightning Source UK Ltd.
Milton Keynes UK
UKHW021051161122
412293UK00009B/123